LETS
GO
PUBLISH!

Double Whammy: Incompetence & Corruption in Public School Governance Volume II of II

Chronicle of Inept Governance & Corrective Actions

A school board from hell causes a big question: Is there a better way to govern our public school districts?

by
Richard A Holodick, Ph.D.
Brian W. Kelly, M.B.A.

A toxic WB Area school board purchased a toxic site to build a toxic school at a toxic price

Hard as it may be to believe, there are no qualifications to be on a public school board, and there is no compensation. Unless your hand is under the table for some clandestine remuneration, why bother? For the few and far between honest politician, the time commitment is substantial, and the magnitude of responsibility is overwhelming. Criticism is abundant. The operative question follows: "Is there a better way to govern our school districts?"

In volume I, you learned about the actions taken by a democratically elected board of directors whose job it was to manage the affairs of the Wilkes-Barre Area School District on behalf of the public. The people of the district still see this as a struggle for safe, enduring, neighborhood schools. In this Volume II, with the project well underway, the people continue to ask and we continue to help answer the major question of the day: Is there a better way to govern our public school districts?

In this volume, we offer additional proof of poor governance as we offer suggestions for how to make life better for the Wilkes-Barre Area School District and all school districts in the country who seek better governance. In WB Area, and many other districts, this has a sense of urgency because *We can't wait until there are no WB high schools and the tax burden is unsustainable.*

By

Richard A. Holodick, Ph.D. &
Brian W. Kelly, M.B.A

Referenced Material : *Standard Disclaimer: The information in this book has been obtained through personal and third Party observations, interviews, and copious research. Where unique information has been provided or extracted from other sources, those sources are acknowledged within the text of the book itself or at the end of the chapter in the Sources Section. Thus, there are no formal footnotes nor is there a bibliography section. Any picture that does not have a source was taken from various sites on the Internet with no credit attached. If resource owners would like credit in the next printing, please email publisher.*

Published by:	LETS GO PUBLISH!
Editor	Brian P. Kelly
Email:	info@letsgopublish.com
Web site	www.letsgopublish.com

PO Box 621 Wilkes-Barre PA 18703
Library of Congress Copyright Information Pending
Book Cover Design by Richard Holodick & Brian W. Kelly

Acknowledgments are available for viewing at www.letsgopublish.com **at the bottom of the main menu..**

ISBN Information: The International Standard Book Number (ISBN) is a unique machine-readable identification number, which marks any book unmistakably. The ISBN is the clear standard in the book industry. 159 countries and territories are officially ISBN members. The Official ISBN for this book: **978-1-951562-41-0**

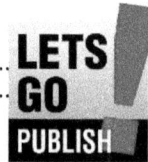

The price for this work is: **$16.95 USD**

10	9	8	7	6	5	4	3	2	1

Release Date: December 2020

Prolog

In volume I and in this book, Volume II, you learn about the actions taken by a democratically elected board of directors whose job it is to manage the affairs of the Wilkes-Barre Area School District on behalf of the public. Additionally, your authors leverage their experience with the local school board to offer solutions to the governance issues that are prevalent in School Districts across the country.

Unfortunately, in this book and through other sources, you will also learn that this board is like many others in the country, who, though duly elected by the people, proceeded to mislead the very same people about their intentions in governance. In fact, without a proper governance model, they misrepresented themselves by agreeing, if elected, to represent the people and provide for the needs of the students above all else. Obviously your authors would not have felt the need to write these two volumes if our local board had kept its promises.

Renderings of what we call the Big Toxic School at Little Chernobyl are shown below:

The story is too big to tell it all, but we tell most of it in this book. We will cite quotations from citizens subject to the board's dictates to make our point. You will see that this board has chosen to follow what many would say is a legitimate governance plan but it can only be concluded that it was an inept course of action which went against the known wishes of the people of the area, which they had sworn to serve.

Board Members Don't Plan To Fail

They Failed To Plan *A Curriculm/Facility Long Range Master Plan*

Please note: The contents of this book are critical to the past boards and this sitting board. The exceptions to this are the Save Our Schools backed new board members—Terry Schiowitz, and Beth Ann Owens Harris and board member Missi Patla.

The essence of the issue in dispute is whether perfectly maintainable and well-built and historically relevant neighborhood school structures in the City of Wilkes-Barre should be abandoned, discarded, and torn down so that the board can build its idea of Taj Mahal school on top of a toxic mine dump, in a community outside the major city in the school district. It is rare when a board operates against the best interests of its major municipality. Their callous action has left Wilkes-Barre City (WB) with no high schools from three.

The board has determined that the City which makes up over 60% of the school district simply does not matter. Though it will hurt businesses and property owners in Wilkes-Barre City, the board has remained indifferent to the plight of over 60% of its taxpayers. City taxpayers and officials are expected to give up all of its high schools for this board's potential hazardous folly. For over 100 years, these three WB City High Schools have met the needs of the students and the taxpayers in City high schools named Coughlin, GAR, and Meyers.

Coughlin   G.A.R.   Meyers

The current board clearly has not served its constituents well and has shut the public out of the major decision making. Volume II of this two volume work covers the problems with school district governance. Consider that the caretakers of $300 million in real estate assets has never had a maintenance plan.

In other words, they had no plan for the upkeep of school buildings for over the past fifty years if ever. They have no qualified staff to provide maintenance work in any of the $300,000,000 worth of properties, which are "owned" by the school district. Why is this so important?

If the board had the proper team of in-house builders, and maintainers, and a plan for them to do their jobs regularly, keeping the properties maintained, there would not have been a perceived "urgent" need to replace the three historically relevant, well-built high schools in Wilkes- Barre City with an abomination constructed outside the City limits on top of a toxic mine shaft.

The only planning of this "independent" board, over the citizens objections, is to tear down these historical structures because as trustees of district property, they exercised a one-word board maintenance philosophy of neglect, neglect, and neglect, repeated three times for effect.

The board failed and they are preparing to fail again. The board's dream school should not be built because the old is far better than the new. Well-built forever schools should never be replaced. Granite and marble, major ingredients in the three high schools. do not dissipate and decay over time.

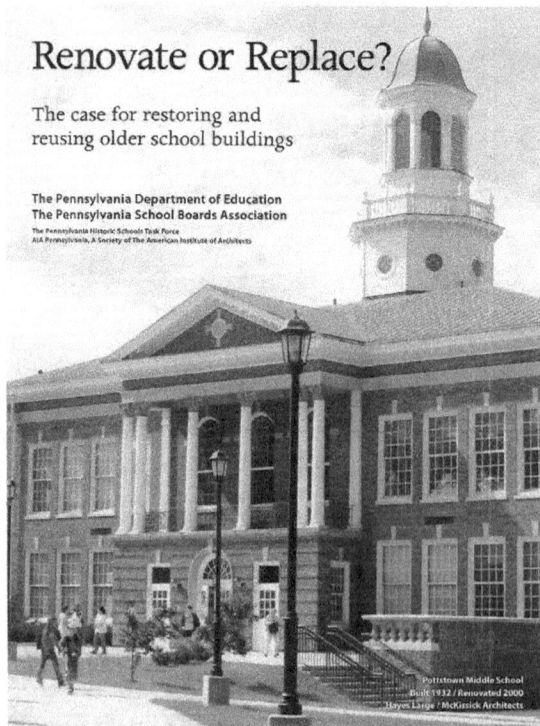

Renovate or Replace?

The case for restoring and reusing older school buildings

The Pennsylvania Department of Education
The Pennsylvania School Boards Association

The Pennsylvania Historic Schools Task Force
AIA Pennsylvania, A Society of The American Institute of Architects

Pottstown Middle School
Built 1932 / Renovated 2000
Hayes Large / McKissick Architects

It is difficult to understand building new when major authoritative agencies have published for School Districts to renovate, not to rebuild. Here are some of the authorities recommending this strategy:

- The American Institute of Architects (AIA)
- The Pennsylvania Department of Education School District's Advisors
- The Pa. School Boards Association
- The Pa. Historical Society support renovations.

Considering the historical society, which finds great historical value in the three WB high schools, think about this. If our esteemed WBA Board had been around two centuries ago, would Independence Hall have survived? Would the WBASB have torn down Independence Hall and got rid of Philadelphia's most historic structure? I bet they would have.

Writing for Smithsonian, Whitey Martinko in December 2017 suggested: "Goodbye Independence Hall, hello Amazon headquarters! He noted that the parody website *onion* had lampooned Philadelphia's eagerness to house Amazon's second command center and included an image of the city leveled to make way for this new business.

Nobody knows what the real motivations were for the board to abandon Wilkes-Barre, but at least it was not for Amazon. Most think it was worse—corruption and greed, plus there was a particular superintendent whose pride was hurt when the SOS group beat him on the Washington Street Zoning.

Whatever the reason, the WBA Board made a dumb decision. It is a mistake the people of the area will be paying for, until they find their graves. Thankfully WBA's board did not get a vote on Independence Hall or it too would be gone along with Coughlin, GAR, and Meyers high schools.

Should a major city face neighborhood blight by removing three major reasons for people to live there. Besides the folly of the idea itself, the site they picked is toxic. No kidding! There ought to be a law. Maybe there is and the Save our Schools (SOS) group is looking for it.

Despite grave warnings of children and staff potentially getting sick on toxic waste from the new school site, this board chose to place the health of students at risk. What esteemed body working for the public good would subject those learning or working at Mine Shaft High in Little Chernobyl from the toxic material, toxic water, and toxic fumes from the designed school built on top of a hazardous waste dump.

More and more citizens of the WB Area believe we were duped into believing the words of the Consigliere that putting poor Wilkes-Barre Area citizens in debt up to a half billion or more dollars after the State's contribution, was the only solution to having children well-educated in this area. Soon the foreclosure teams from the county and other taxing bodies will be coming for all the properties of the elderly who will not be able to pay the massive taxes required for the board's Taj Mahal. Citizens of WB Area, there is no need for this monstrosity. SOS is trying to find a law and we could use your help.

Dedication

This book is dedicated to the long-suffering citizens of Wilkes-Barre Area, having endured the tyranny of their elected self-centered school board for far too long

In this endeavor, your authors, Richard A. Holodick and Brian W. Kelly are individual members of the Save Our Schools Group. They are serving in this publishing endeavor as instruments of public awareness.

This book is a private work product of Dr. Holodick & Mr. Kelly and was not commissioned by or sponsored by the Save Our Schools Committee.

You and your friends may download Volume I of the book at no charge for three months after its availability.
http://www.letsgopublish.com/files/littlechernobylnotok.pdf

Order Book 1 through Amazon at this direct URL:
https://www.amazon.com/dp/1951562305/

Order Book 2 through Amazon at this direct URL:
https://www.amazon.com/dp/XXXXXXXXXXXX

Acknowledgments

Chronicle of Inept Governance & Corrective Actions:

A school board from hell causes a big question:
Is there a better way to govern our public school districts?

by
Richard A Holodick, Ph.D.
Brian W. Kelly, M.B.A.

A toxic WB Area school board purchased a toxic site to build a toxic school

Please don't forget that first and foremost nearly all evidence says don't consolidate schools because it harms academics, student sense of well-being, student participation, and that it increases costs. Having said that, the building site is receiving such attention because outside of perhaps Chernobyl, it would be difficult to find a worse spot to build a school.

Dr. Holodick and Mr. Kelly would like to publicly acknowledged all of the help that we have received from many sources. Certain chapters and parts of this two book set are written by other authors and are cited in place.

Preface

School Boards, Directors, and Trustees

As required by the Pennsylvania School Code, public school districts are governed by a School Board that is comprised of directors/trustees who serve terms. In compliance with state and federal laws, school boards establish policies and regulations by which their schools are governed.

The daily operation of a school district from small, medium to large sized district can be compared to the operation of a business. For this publication we focused on the Wilkes Barre Area School District. A school district that encompasses 124 square miles, the city and surrounding communities.

In the confines of this area, sixty-seven thousand residents are at the poverty level. The student population is just under seven thousand students. The employee count of the district, full and part time is nearly 1000. The district includes nine separate facilities.

The WBA School District contracts out the bussing of students. Its operating budget exceeds $121 million dollars per annum, which by state reg Code 609 must not be overspent. This paragraph establishes that this district is a large business. The traditional superintendent (CEO) graduates from high school, enters college, earning a teacher's degree and teaches. He/she forwards his/her education earning a masters and doctorate degree with an accompanying "Letter of Eligibility" certification to hold a superintendent's position.

The missing component is private sector experience running a business or even working in the private sector. This is a serious concern as the superintendent is responsible for running a large business. Being a teacher or a director of curriculum does not help in the experience column as private businesses have no such positions.

The real-world experience of a superintendent without private business experience can be aided by the election of board members with real world experience and dedication to meeting the mission of a public school, which as we know is to "educate and inspire."

Looking at our subject in both volumes of this report, the WBA school board, it appears that it is a textbook, typical board. There are four retired WBA administrators with master's degrees, a minister, who is African American, and a handicapped grandparent, graduate of the district. Why then if the components seem to be OK is the governance of the whole not working?

The missing piece is that there is no bible. There is no policies and procedures manual. And, so it can be proven that the board has no policies/ procedures for the board's operation. There is no bible for operations nor is there a Roberts Rules of Order which helps guide the movements of this group of individuals.

If it were not for nepotism and cronyism being clearly evident in the hiring results, there would be no discernable set of rules by which the board uses as its de-facto operating prescription . Neglect is the only visible maintenance philosophy. These features, coupled with practices that flaunt the employment, promotion, and the contracting with the inexperienced, results in what one would expect—failure.

There is no one held responsible--even the Superintendent is blameless for the low academic ranking except the un-connected...all three of them. Yes, with a superintendent who just had his contract renewed, the district is ranked closer to the very bottom within the bottom 50% of all 704 school districts in Pennsylvania (based off of combined math and reading proficiency testing data) In the 2017-2018 school year for example, the school district's graduation rate of 85% decreased from 88% over the prior five school years.

Accountability for internal and external contracted services is non-existent at zero percent.. The district is in dire straits with students ranked at the bottom statewide in academics, PFM [What is PFM and why is it important] study predicted a $70 million- dollar deficit, and 8 of the nine facilities are old and need of replacement or renovations. The price tag to make the district whole can reach a HALF BILLIION dollars. They have begun massive costly project(s) including the Big Toxic School consolidation at the Little Chernobyl site in Plains Twp. without as much as a curriculum/facility long range master plan. This publication describes what the fallout has been and it adds some protocols for what needs to take place moving forward.

Unfortunately for the citizens of Wilkes-Barre Area, our school board, which was elected in good faith by the citizens, believes it was elected to hold office so it could serve its own selfish agenda. The members have chosen to disregard the will of the people. They do not believe in the precepts brought forth by the founders. Instead they have made their governance all powerful instead of being subservient to the people as it is written in law.

Board members ~~almost~~ vehemently object to being referred to as corrupt. Yet, an objective analysis would surely prove otherwise. Whether the WBASB is a corrupt enterprise may very well be a matter of opinion. This book will present facts to help you make the decision for yourself.

We have researched the Roslyn School District so that we would know what school district corruption looks like and what it smells like. There are those in Wilkes-Barre Area who think it looks like this school district and the WBA School District has a smell that suggests it is not 100% pure and clean.

Back in 2019, on a weekend later in that year, HBO released its story of "Bad Education." This film was led by Hugh Jackman-and just as if it were a story about the Wilkes-Barre Area School District (WBASD), it is about a real life school district and a serious school board scandal involving a lot of money. It took place about two decades ago in a place very unlike WBASD in that it is an affluent suburb of Long Island.

In the movie Frank Tassone, the Superintendent played by Jackman is portrayed as a successful, charismatic superintendent of the Roslyn School District in Roslyn, New York. He was loved and trusted much like some of the characters in our WBASD story.

The difference is that in his role as top dog, Tassone goes on to steal $11.2 million from the school budget with his associate Pamela Gluckin. In Bad Education, Gluckin is played by Oscar winner Allison Janney). This turns out to be a story about the largest public school embezzlement in U.S. history. Of course folks, the WBASD story has really not yet been fully told.

Though our story and their story both smell bad and are a lot alike in many ways, there is no loot that has been found stashed in any of the story characters homes or school lockers or bank accounts. Some observers of Wilkes-Barre Area Officials and the Board may add a key word to this summary: "YET!"

The Founders knew that even the great Constitution they wrote might not be enough to keep knaves and scoundrels from subverting their work. We see the personification of everything the bad notions from which the Founders attempted to protect us in the current Wilkes-Barre Area School Board. I wish it were different but it is what it is.

Here we are 230+ years after the Constitution was ratified. All is not perfect in America, nor is it perfect in the burgs and cities and towns that make up the individual parts of America. Nonetheless, the principles of the Constitution are so sound and so powerful that even a knave politician cannot bring our country or any municipality down—even though they may try. Eventually, like Frank Tassone they get caught.

Our tyrannical school board cannot and will not stand. The people will prevail. Voting every two years for new board members, the people will have another opportunity to win back control of their school board next year. Your authors can assure the people that a vote for the Save our Schools (SOS) slate of candidates will be a breath of fresh air for the people and that says it all

We have all learned from our recent experience that there are far too many politicians who today control the Wilkes-Barre Area School Board (WBASB). Their mission is to overthrow the will of the people and impose their will upon us. You will learn about them in this two-volume book. The big concern in Wilkes-Barre Area, of course is that if we don't smarten up, things can and will get a lot worse. Nobody expects a school board dictatorship amidst a democracy / republic. I suspect that is why you are reading this book.

Your intention no doubt in learning about the issues of the people v the WBASB has to do with how the people who knowingly voted in these candidates and officials, who now rule by tyranny, can come up with a solution to minimize the great power that they gave away to these knaves in past elections. We can do it unless we give up! Let's not give up!

By choosing to read this book, you have decided that you want to understand why what is happening regarding this area of the country is happening. Thank you. That is why Richard Holodick and Brian Kelly wrote this book and why the members of the SOS team are so glad that we all may eventually understand what is happening.

Holodick and Kelly wrote this book so that the people of Wilkes-Barre Area can know the stakes of having an incompetent and incorrigible board in office. They wrote this book so that the people will always be able to make the correct decisions on representation in the future. Thank you for reading this book.

For anybody else out there who can help us make this right, we will accept your help. For example we would welcome help from Erin Brockavich, who knows how to win against powerful forces of evil. We would be glad to accept help from Mike Makowski, who wrote the screen play for Bad Education. We'd also accept support from Hugh Jackman, Ray Romano, and Allison Janney, and Welker White, the actors and actresses who starred in *Bad Education*. Their experience taught them a lot and we need their help.

Wilkes-Barre Area needs a great screen play from Makowski and great actors and actresses to represent our area in its fight against tyranny. And, of course we could use a dose of the gristle and the guts of the real Erin Brockovich whose picture is shown on the next page.

You are going to love the rest of this book since it is designed by two Americans for the Americans who are living in the Wilkes-Barre Area. Few books are a must-read but *Little Chernobyl* is destined to quickly appear at the top of Northeastern Pennsylvania's and the nation's most read list.

Sincerely,

Brian P. Kelly, Editor in Chief on behalf of Authors Richard Holodick and Brian Kelly

Table of Contents

About the Author, Richard Holodick

The photo above was taken 1938, mother with her first child. The second photo is a post card 1938, of Elmer L. Meyers High School, Mother, Gertrude Zupa would be in the first graduating class, at Meyers son Richard the 1956 graduating class, Meyers High School. Richard born with a physical handicap brought on by a toxic, who would endure classmates bulling because he was different, and experience 16 corrective surgeries, and years of speech therapy. **Perhaps bringing forth a passion for stopping a school from being constructed on a toxic dump.**

I would be advised by certified counselors that my academic deficiencies would negate post-secondary level schooling. And, a speech impediment, discouraged public speaking. Seek a trade they said, I did, working as an electrician for the International Brotherhood of Electrical Workers. This led to a teaching position requiring daily group speaking, and college work that I was told to stupid to handle; graduate level GPA 3.6. Long story short, degrees from three universities, a Ph.D. earned through a national scholarship, U.S. Department of Education: PSU master's in administration via PDE state grant. Set professional goals, to work at the secondary, community college and university levels of education, providing a diverse work experience to match the diverse education acquired at three universities. I added to diversity by working in four states. I attribute my achievements to a diverse education, diverse work experience, professional consultant, and substantial private sector experience.

A statewide search by Penn State brought me my university level experience, main campus where I also earned a master's degree in administration, free. Another national search led to an associate Dean position in Colorado at a community college. A U.S Assistant Secretary of Education, serving prior as a superintendent in Oklahoma City School District hired me as his assistant following a national search. I was promoted to Superintendent two years later.

I responded to a national search for a director of planning for City Colleges of Chicago, was selected. On the national level I worked 20 years part time consulting for an international curriculum/facility master planning firm.

Local assignments were at the Luzerne County Community College where I wrote educational and equipment specifications for the High Technology Center, Misericordia University, writing the educational and equipment specifications for the renovation of the science and nursing programs. I have presented at state and national conferences. Awarded millions in grant writing for serving the needs of at-risk children and adults. Concluded my career serving five years in jail; Director of Education at the State Correctional institutions at Camp Hill and Dallas Pa.

Professional certifications, Superintendent Oklahoma. Pa, Vocational-Technical Director, High School Principal, I. U. Executive Director, electrical construction instructor, and cooperative education coordinator. All the above was the motivation for wanting to see WBA 7000 students off the bottom ranking in academics, a district in dire straits financially, and aged, neglected restorable historic facilities. I have published in the National Correctional Journal, on my dissertation." Competences Needed to teach in Correctional Facilities." And at age 83 just completed co-authoring two books on corruption in the Wilkes-Barre School District, and "Chronicle of Inept Governance & Corrective Actions" at the WBASD.

About the Author, Brian W. Kelly

Brian W. Kelly has a B.S. in Data Processing / Computer Science and an MBA in Accounting and Finance. He retired as an Assistant Professor in the Business Information Technology (BIT) program at Marywood University, where he also served as the IBM i and midrange systems technical advisor to the IT faculty. Kelly designed, developed, and taught many college and professional courses. He is a contributing technical editor to a number of IT industry magazines. On the patriotic side, you can find many of Kelly's articles on www.brianwkelly.com. He is a major author for Lets Go Publish! – www.letsgopublish.com

Kelly is a former IBM Senior Systems Engineer and in his post technical career, he has been a candidate for US Congress and the US Senate from Pennsylvania. He also ran for Mayor of Wilkes-Barre. Not being a politician, Brian learned from his losses that it is very difficult to fight the machine,

Kelly has an active information technology consultancy. He is the author of 260 books and numerous articles. Ask Brian to speak at your next rally! You would enjoy his frank perspectives! Over the past twenty five years, Brian has become the most published non-fiction author in America and one of America's most outspoken and eloquent conservative / nationalist protagonists. Brian loves America. Besides *The Electoral College 4 Dummmies*, Kelly is also the author of many other patriotic books. Check them out at www.Amazon.com /author/brianwkelly, Kindle, Barnes & Noble and other fine online booksellers.

Plot Preview

The SOS Group has long been fighting the Wilkes-Barre Area School Board (WBASB) hoping to gain a decision to turn around the notion of eliminating all three historically relevant high schools in Wilkes-Barre City. Though it is late in the game with the building construction continuing, residents of WBA have never given up the fight. "What's bad is bad and time will only make it worse." The Big Toxic School at Chernobyl is bad and the situation is getting worse but we are better with a late solution than none at all.

Dr. Richard Holodick, and Brian W. Kelly wrote this two volume book to help the board know the right thing to do and then to do the right thing. Holodick and Kelly want to "keep the idea alive that it is not good to risk the health of teenagers by sending the children of Wilkes-Barre Area to a Toxic School." Across the country such practices are banned because building over toxic waste has been proven to be unsafe and very dangerous for the public's health, especially the young school students.

Dr. Richard Holodick is president of Save Our Schools, a major opposition group formed to oppose the consolidation of high schools in the Wilkes-Barre Area School District. Holodick, 83, is a 1956 graduate of Wilkes-Barre's Meyers High School. He retired from a lengthy career as an educator in 2001 and he lives in Wilkes-Barre. His expertise is school district governance and he has offered the school district his pro-bono expertise to help turn the WBA's fortunes around to positive.

Holodick has had a distinguished career exemplified by the successes in the many institutions he has assisted. For example, The City Colleges of Chicago wanted a $60 million dollar high tech center. They performed a national search and hired Holodick. City Colleges of Chicago is one of the largest systems in the US, nine facilities serve 77,000 students a year. In another national search, he was selected by a former US Assistant Secretary of Education to start a new school district. Despite his distinguished successes, he did not meet the education and experience to be appointed to a WBA board seat for which he aspired, twice.

All-in-all, Holodick has been an effective leader in the education industry for over 30 years in four states. He is an impressive human being. His co-author, Brian Kelly could not have begun to write a book about school district governance and we can all thank Dr. Holodick for his major contributions to this effort.

Holodick has served as assistant superintendent and as superintendent in major school districts. He was an Associate Dean at Aims Community College and a full-time project director at Penn State Main campus. He served as the Director of Education for the State Correctional Institution at Dallas Pa. He served as an Educational consultant with accolades for the Paullin Group Inc., an international curriculum/facility master planning firm. Working with this expert gives his coworkers the knowledge that Dr. Richard Holodick is the epitome of extreme competence.

Like most of the SOS group which Dr. Holodick leads, he is involved in all the battles as the group's principle spokesman. And, there are quite a few battles going on, all of which are important to the residents and taxpayers of the District. First of all WB Area is a poverty district and cannot afford the Taj Mahal school which is expected to cost about a half billion dollars over forty years. Wilkes-Barre City, with a declining population to begin, will lose its remaining population and will no longer be able to attract industry as its three high schools are eliminated and demolished. What businesses would be attracted with pictures and accounts of a wrecking ball tearing down the only high schools in the major city in the district. . Businesses look to cities where there is a construction crane signifying business activity.

Moreover, the possibility of neighborhood schools and community-based learning, the preferred vehicle in the modern era is eliminated 100% with the movement to a huge consolidated school in which no child is important. Additionally and probably the worst of all situations is that the project site as you will learn was selected more to spite Wilkes-Barre and rushed through without the necessary precautions for the safety of the children, faculty and staff who will breathe the air in the Big Toxic School at Little Chernobyl.

In his role as President of SOS, as noted Dr. Holodick writes many newspaper columns and letters to the editor. As consolidation project is at the half way point or as some say, it is in its eleventh hour, nobody from SOS, the least of whom would be Dr. Richard Holodick has given up. It is just too important .

Despite the fact that the Wilkes-Barre Area School Board (WBASB) has remained fixed and quite rigid in not accepting input from the community, the people and SOS continue to send in the volleys. To no apparent avail. WBA has the epitome of bad governance in the membership body of this board. And, so, in his own words, Dr. Holodick composed this "Hail Mary" appeal to the board hoping they will end their intransigence and decide to work with SOS for the betterment of the community at large.

Here is the preamble to his editorial:

Preamble

There are 67,000 residents, with a high percentage of seniors (76%), 6800 students, 76% of the residents are in the economically disadvantaged and at- risk category, nearly 1000 full and part employees, and a city, which is also the county seat, attempting to recover: all desperately needing your help! If you care and importantly realize the awesome responsibility of the WBA school board at this critical time, half billion-dollar undertaking and dealing with a pandemic,

YOU NEED TO READ THIS PAPER TWICE.

PLEASE do not make the mistake that this is over because the building is 50% complete, it's a beginning. Yes, the new three high school consolidation may have had its ribbon cutting. But the fact is the site that may well be capped and stay capped is still an at-risk site that will require constant monitoring as per EPA.

We await the PDE Plan Con hearing and an investigation by the Department of the Interior, Washington DC on the DEP's monitoring of the fracking industry. The Auditor General stated that "the monitoring by DEP was based on the size of a wallet or connections." [FYI that means the inspectors would have their hands out for graft.] Damn right scary! site. Then there is the need to address the academic and financial needs and the requirements for six aged schools. Short- and long-range planning is a mandate as it is in all school districts that are well managed..

Respectably, CREDIBILITY with credentials. I need you to believe what I have to say about this dire situation. I have degrees from three universities. Ph.D. was awarded through a US Department of Education scholarship. Experience at the secondary, community college, and university levels, assistant superintendent of a 40,000 student, 5000 employee district that bussed 12,000 students, City College of Chicago, Director of Planning, 77,000 students a year in 9 facilities. Twenty years plus consulting for the Pa, Department of Education, and an international facility, master planning firm, Grand Rapids Mi; completed assignments for Misericordia University, the Luzerne County Community College and the Perry Traditional Academy, Pittsburgh School District.

Here is the report:

The State of the WBASD
Presented to: The Wilkes-Barre Area School Board RE: A call for immediate action
By: Richard A. Holodick, Ph.D.

The education, safety, self and school pride, of 7000 students, 76% of 67,000 residents, faculty and staff, a city, and the very survival of the public education as we have known it, is at stake. The "Mission Statement" for the district "To Educate and Inspire," is far from being accomplished, but reachable. In addition, the non- discrimination policy, "... does not discriminate," was violated and continues.

The infamous nepotism/cronyism the community talks about freely is alive and well. Previous boards have had serious credibility problems stemming from fraud that jailed four of them. The most recent was a board president (Elmy). He faced a life sentence in prison for of all thing's extortion. The present board also has credibility problems, perhaps not equal to past boards; but pending? "Public Trust" has been seriously violated. During this criminal's tenure (Elmy) as president the board exceeded the operational budget by $10 million—a violation of law 609.

To gain support and a major reference point, we turn to a nationally known public education reformer, one of the best in the country.

Dr. Terry Grier

The picture above is of two-time Superintendent of the Year and Lifelong Educator, *Dr. Terry Grier*. Among his major achievements, Dr. Grier is known for this quote:

"If you don't have a great school board, you're not going to have a great school district."

Think about that folks. Not only is the board leadership important, but the superintendent, building principals and teachers. Grier touts a groundbreaking formula that he used to improve the seventh largest district in the country. His formula and methodologies earn him national recognition as *a reformer*.

Leadership, rigor, accountability, choice and community engagement are reoccurring themes for this outstanding school reformer. There was a time when the WBASD had impeccable credentials and results: This quote is from The Times Leader in 1968:

"The City school district standards are among the highest in the country."

Ladies and Gentlemen, it can be duplicated.

I bring to the table fifty years in four states; twenty years part time consulting for an international facility/master planning firm; I am no Dr. Grier but I consider myself a reformer. With the assistance of David Wilson, school choice, community engagement (SOS), the district's task force committees, the district's feasibility study, the PFM study, and scholarly research, this school district can be returned to the days of national academic and facility recognition and major acclaim.

Additionally, by addressing the issues that are obvious, it can save the taxpayers in this poverty ridden district a hundred million dollars and perhaps more over the next 40 years. You see it's all here no reinventing the wheel, just listen and follow through. Where there is a will, there is a way.

If you always listen to who you always listened to you, will always get what you always got. The board has been advised by their novice superintendent, their solicitor, and their construction management firm. Nothing of value in life is free. From January 2020 to April 2020, the monthly costs for such services were:

- Apollo $66,833 (monthly average)
- Superintendent $16,000 a month, salary, $148,000 year
- Solicitor $19,000a month, contract, $195,000 year

To use an agrarian analogy, these are not small potatoes.

Even though some know the numbers, I'll bet that they surprise many and that you have been adding them up in your head from the mini-chart above.

Well, if you have your math right, you already know that this EQUALS a cost of Over a HUNDRED THOUSAND DOLLARS A MONTH. With a six-month average, most of us would go broke, yet we the taxpayers pay this as required by contract.

The monthly average expenditure would be close + or – which would equal over the past 4 years nearly $5 million for "advice." In all fairness it included the salary of a novice superintendent's running the district. If the board chose to look for expertise rather than hire the default players from the last team with a poor record, you might be surprised.

A highly experienced superintendent, full time solicitor, and full-time construction manager could be employed for far less than a hundred thousand dollars a month. If you did not know that, you now do. The District has not been shopping well as far better choices are available and compared to the prices being paid, thee are major personnel bargains to be had. Of course this is only germane if the board wishes to minimize taxpayer expense.

Right within the group known as Save Our Schools are several outstanding people who have examined the decisions of the board in terms of expenses and find them wanting. Dr. Holodick, David Wilson, the Borland's, as well as internal and external task force committees could help change this district's academic success and facility needs in three to four years and save the district a hundred million dollars over a 40-year span.

The cost for such advice from those identified who can assist and almost assure success is ZERO.

The public has access to the board minutes and other communications and those who ready this material already know that the public is being shortchanged.

For example, they know that the hundred thousand a month advice yielded these inadequate results for the people of WBA:

- Poor advice said that omitting the high school with the highest percentage of minorities and economically disadvantaged students from "the new school" was deemed acceptable, and not considered the decision segregation. In this case, the novice superintendent swore under oath, "GAR students would not be in the new school, and if WB does not want us in the city we will move out."
  - The NAACP response to the Super: "Racism is alive and well."

- Poor advice said that sending a plan to PDE Plan Con Division to build a consolidated large school on 2.7 acres, when the state recommends 35 acres, and where zoning prohibits public schools would be acceptable—yet it was not!.
- Poor advice said that there was no need to hold off expenditures that exceeded $6 million, to wait to see if a zoning waiver (Coughlin & Kistler projects) was granted; it failed. Yet, the funds were wasted because of board ego.

- Poor advice said that renovating an elementary school built for 500 students and not expanding an existing highs school with room, was prudent and though built for 500 elementary students, the advice suggested 800 high school students would fit. The plan failed.

- Advice suggested that the district should rejecting the Murray Complex site simply because it bordered a railroad tracks, and was next to a busy street. Yet, a site next to the Cross Valley Express Way, bordering a railroad, unlined coal ash dump, industrial waste dump, with a history of subsidence was deemed safer for WBASD children. The Board Solicitor, one of those offering advice on the project affirmed that our children would have to eat the coal ash to be harmed. His statement can be reproduced from board minutes.

- Poor advice stated that it is ok to spend taxpayer's dollars to improve land that is not owned by the taxpayers. When the board and superintendent had ruled out the city of Wilkes-Barre, the district's wallet opened to spend as much as needed so that Wilkes-Barre would regret not offering zoning for an inadequate city site.

- In this regard, State law requires the owner to reclaim the land prior to selling. The board nonetheless used taxpayer dollars because of its vendetta v the WB zoning office to pay whatever was the price to get out of the city so the Super approved the purchase of the land un- reclaimed, costing the taxpayers millions of unnecessary expenditures.

- Poor advice recommended a board action which required the purchase of the Pagnotti site at the appraised value. Looking at the results, this meant that the taxpayer's paid 5 times the lowest assessed value, $10,000 an acre, purchased for $55,000 an acre based on mineral rights that were not included in the deeds and were never appraised. The justification of $55,000 an acre based on $50,000 an acre paid for the Valley Crest site that was deep mined. However, it never had a subsidence prone designation, it was never a coal ash dump, it was not an industrial waste dump, and it had a substantial infrastructure. Why would the advice suggest this? Why would the board take the advice?

- The trio's advice recommended the rejection of a donation of 55 acres because "it was too costly to build on." It was donated by Geisinger a well-known and prestigious hospital. It was a toxic free site, with a sound infrastructure. It was subsidence free and FREE to own without issues for the children. Why?

- Why did the advice suggest spending $3 million on Coughlin refurbishing and turn around and sell for $1.8 million.

- Why did the advice suggest that the original plan was to demolish and remove historic Meyers High School for $13 million and have an empty lot worth a half million.

- Why did the advice suggest that it was OK to ignore the district's second major problem of six aged unkept facilities; and agree to lease a 90-year-old building, Times leader for $50,000 a month. Why were there no outside people permitted to counsel the board ?

- Why did the advisors suggest that in a poverty ridden district, underfunded by $33 million a year enter a project that exceeds a quarter of a BILLION dollars over forty years to serve 2400 students, leaving 4600 students housed in aged facilities? How is this prudent?

- Why would the advisors believe it was financially prudent to select a site what required 95% of the students having to be bussed when in the alternatives only 35% of the students had to take the bus to school.

The advisors and the board who were advised had access to many studies exceeding a million dollars that stated closing neighborhood schools was a "disadvantage." The same reports offered that creating a middle school was a bad idea. Why did the advisors recommend closing all neighborhood high schools and against outside advice, build two middle schools.

Knowing what we now know and what we knew at the onset of the consolidation project for Little Chernobyl, would anybody suggest that the Pagnotti site was the best site to build a school for our children.

These factors were in our own studies. However, in addition, we know that scholarly research predicts substandard outcomes for the demographics of the students we serve that are at the 76% at risk factors.

Considering curriculum changes for academic success, and a half billion-dollar fix over a 40-year period, and no one in the hundred thousand dollar a month advisory club—the big three earners—said that we need a long-range curriculum/facility master plan? Why? Why not?

Another missing tool was impact studies. Let's take a time out to explain the notion of an impact study and what its value would be in this project. Quite simply an impact study is a management tool used in the public and private sector. Some call it a kind of a "what if." Let me explain. We will review the notion of an impact study in later chapters. For now, the following should suffice.

When there is an idea that develops into a plan to accomplish a goal-- for example if the board decides to close a high school, an impact study would assess its impact and determine where to locate 800 students. This is what happened in WBA in its renovation and use of the Mackin School which had been a shuttered elementary school.

There was no impact study—just a quick off the cuff plan to supposedly fit 800 students from Coughlin High School in a 500-student facility. Since even a shoehorn could not accomplish this, the board was forced to use split schedule, without knowing the impact or ramifications of its hurried decision.

The result would be that in order to pull off what was a bad idea to start, the school day would stretch to 12 hours. There was little consideration to the fact that the area around the school is congested, and so on. Had an impact study been done, it would have been found that these students could be accommodated at Meyers High School. The poorly conceived plan was quickly put together to consolidate Coughlin and Meyers high schools.

Another example is the board erroneously concluded without an impact study that consolidation was in the WBASD's best intersts. It was supposedly going to save the taxpayer's money by reducing the # of high schools into one. This decision was not thought out and was against what the board had previously determined was the best course of action for the district—i.e. neighborhood schools So, the board made what could be called a non-educational decision:

An impact study would have revealed that to take care of the 7th through 12th grade with a consolidated school designed for 9th through 12th, two facilities would be required—a new "consolidated school" and a middle school. GAR was quickly reworked to become a middle school. The idea of saving money on consolidation was compromised because there ws no impact study that would bring all the costs to the light of day before making the decision.

Total costs of renovations, new construction, interest payments and additional bussing killed any possibility of saving the taxpayers money. An impact study would have gathered necessary data from other districts that had successfully performed their consolidations. If none could be found then this fact would have said the impact was not worth the risk.

As noted, the decision to convert GAR to a middle school needed an impact study; impact on the $40 million dollar cost, the fact that our study and research had previously determined middle schools wrre not the best course of action for WBASD and in fact presented themselves as a major disadvantage, etc.

An impact study would have prevented the board's spending $3 million on pre-sale work and putting the building up for sale for less than $2 million on Coughlin when it was determined that the interior needed demolition for the removal of dangerous asbestos. But, strange as it may seem, Coughlin at this time was no longer in the board's plan to be used as a high school. So, why invest?

I think that about covers the notion of an impact study and why it is helpful in decision evaluations. A shortened explanation of an impact study can be implemented when board action is needed to change or improve a situation The study would be conducted to determine what ramifications would accompany the change, including cost and impact on students and stakeholders? Impact studies can save a lot of taxpayers dollars by calling attention to and preventing unneeded actions.

Let me rehash this one more time for "impact." A prime example of this is the closing of Coughlin High School without an impact study. The board haphazardly (perhaps they were advised by contractors or paid employees) placed 800 students in a 500-student facility; in a neighborhood that would have difficulty handling the traffic flow. To accommodate this rube Goldberg approach to facilities management, they had to extend the school day while at the same time reducing the actual number of classroom hours. This is what consultants would refer to as a lose-lose proposition.

Of course, there are more errors and omissions, and other areas of bad advice and no advice. but the point has been made that either poor advice, or no advice or a combination of both was provided to the board. Perhaps there were cautions but the board majority just didn't listen. This recalcitrant board typically does as it pleases.

We all know that this scenario is completely unacceptable in a district at the poverty level and underfunded by the state to the tume of $33 million a year. A consolidation and 70% enrollment in Toxic High will undoubtedly bankrupt the school district, educationally and financially, as the debt service will be impossible for WBA to meet.

Besides its innate toxicity. this site has many other disadvantages. For example Little Chernobyl does not have easy access and there is still not a bussing plan to pick up 2000+ students and return them. In addition to the busses, you have student and employees, and delivery trucks.

It's time to look at what cannot be disputed relating to the Wilkes-Barre Area School District. It is a fact that the district reached national prominence in 1968, and it has the honor of graduating a Nobel Prize recipient, Edward B. Lewis. The readily available data today paints a much different story. It displays a series of errors and omissions that has this district among the worse in the state, perhaps the nation if a comprehensive historical review were ever done.

In this two-volume book set, we address the fall from the prominence of academic leadership nationally to the near bottom academically statewide today. Residents and students have a right to ask, "what happened?" The biggest change was haphazard governance . We add to the mix board fraud, nepotism, cronyism--relating to hiring practices, and awarded of contracted services through the pay to play protocol and we find the culprit—bad management.

This major fault not only does not stop the errors, it allows them to grow worse and fester while nobody- from employees to contracted services are held accountable.

It is a fact?

It is sometimes hard to look in the mirror when the face looking back does not look so good. The mirror does not lie when things are not going so well. Despite the mirror shock if that may be the case, there is little learned without a long look at yourself. Here are some facts that anybody taking a long look would find in the Wilkes-Barre Area School District. This is our school district and we elected the caretakers who brought us to where we are. that we

- The district can be considered at the poverty level and yet it is underfunded by the state $33 million a year. Why was more diligence not put into utilizing existing buildings as per PDE, PSBA, AIA, and the Historical Society? Those who tour Meyers and Gar for example are blown away at the elegance of the design and the expensive marble and granite interior materials. They are "forever schools,: yet somehow somebody declared them dead, lifeless, and worthy of demolition. Why? The district's TEAM, with zero experience in large school restoration determined it was too expensive. The publics' request to seek a second opinion along with many other second opinions was denied by the board.

- The academic standing is 443$^{rd.}$ out of 501 school districts. There is no cause and effect and no accountability to the building and school operation owners—the taxpayers . It is hard to believe with such poor academic results and with such a poor record of building maintenance, the employees responsible for the malaise have been given nice raises and promotions.

- Except for the recently renovated Mackin Elementary school all other district schools do not meet state standards, are aged unkept facilities. Maintenance is one of those words not in the WBASD's dictionary. Look at the disrepair in the three historic high schools. Was anyone, or any agency held accountable?

- Coughlin High school, the oldest historical school in the state was closed without a workable placement of 800+ students. **It took a grandmother and a 14-year-old student telling the board of retired administrators it would not work. The student said, we need more instructional hours not less.** Considering Independence Hall, built in 1753 before the founding of America, is still maintained and in great shape 267 years later. Yet, Coughlin, the major historical school in the state is put out to pasture because it was not maintained as it should have been. By the way, with proper caretakers it is not too late to rehabilitate the City's three High Schools. Many plans to do so have been rejected.

- The renovation, not an expansion of Mackin elementary school sized to house 500 students, to accommodate 800 students, in a congested neighborhood was seriously flawed. **Any STEM student could tell you how stupid that move was.**

- The plan submitted to the Pa. Dept. of Education, that segregated the high school with the highest percentage of minorities and economically disadvantaged children was irresponsible. In fact, its repercussions bordered on the illegal. **Twenty-seven stake holders pleaded to table that costly mistake. Voted on in the high school omitted, while students sang their alma mater. June 10, 2015 GAR HS.**

- The selection of the Washington Street site to build a consolidated school, was the only site that understandably forbade public schools, zoned C-3 Commercial, was questionable. **As per previous statement, twenty-seven people warned the board.**

- Irresponsibly by not waiting for a zoning board decision, the premature spending of $6 million on the two related projects put the full $ 6million in the waste bucket. **Understandably, the zoning waiver failed.**

- **Knowing that the District's second biggest problem is its aged facilities, the board nonetheless agreed to a lease purchase of a 90-year-old building.**

- Returning to the list of sites, the board selected the most hazardous, costly, isolated, subsidence prone 78 acres upon which to build a new school. It is a site that does not exude selection competency. Already it is mocked by the public as a nuclear explosion site and the consolidated school is mocked as The Big Toxic School? The public is not dumb, just lethargic when dealing with an intransigent board. It knows that its tax dollars could be used for better things.

- There is a very plausible theory that the rationale for moving the High Schools out of the largest municipality in the Area, WB City was a clear act of retribution aimed at WB City Officials to spite the City for not granting zoning approval to an unworkable site. **If it looks like a duck. It sure appears in historical context as an act of retribution--moving all high schools from the city, and dissolving the preferred neighborhood schools' concept.** Why else? There were other sites in Wilkes-Barre that would not be mocked as this one is.

- **The PFM study lists busing as a disadvantage. Bussing 35% of the students to 90%.**

- The board agreed to pay $4.2 million for a site that had appraisals at $250,000 to $800,000; based on mineral rights. For some reason, mineral rights were **not** transferred to the district in the deeds. That means, that without the mineral rights the board would pay $55,000 an acre, for land appraised at $10,000 an acre. Why?

- **It took a citizen taking the district to court to prove they agreed to pay $4,2 million based on mineral rights not in the deeds. Why**

- The mineral rights omission was corrected, with a value placed at $3 million, established without a certified assessment, in violation of the board action item requiring assessments. Brings up a question: **Can official approved board actions be ignored?**

- In review of contracts awarded and payments made it appears that the taxpayers were paying to improve, possibly reclaim land the district did not own. **Can taxpayer's money be spent**

to improve land they do not own?

- The site has been designated as a beneficial coal ash dump. Public schools by state law are not allowed 900 feet from a beneficial coal ash dump. Why did all of the officials involved approve the building of this school?

- **Five other states do not allow a public school near a contaminated site, we are on top of a contaminated site.** Why did all of the officials involved approve the building of this school?

- Our own study sponsored by the District concluded that **consolidation is a disadvantage.** So, why did we consolidate?

- The research says consolidation doe**s not save money. Despite the research and the facts, WBASD decides to consolidate to supposedly save money and proceed to spend $40 million to prove ourselves wrong.** So, why did we consolidate?

- Our own study sponsored by the District concluded that **middle schools are a disadvantage; Yet, the plan is to have two middle schools.** So, why did we consolidate?

- The Pa. Department of Education, the Pa. School boards Association, the American Institute of Architects, and the Pa. Historical Society support restoration over new school construction. The research proves that schools built before 1950 are so well built they should be designated as "forever schools." – schools that with regular normal maintenance will last forever. Despite the research and the recommendations by authoritative bodies such as these WBASD chooses to discard three architecturally significant historic high schools, to build a new consolidated toxic school. Why?

My apology for repeating facts, but this matter is so serious that certain facts needed to be repeated. For some this debacle may make a very interesting story. For the people living in the Wilkes-Barre Area, so far, it is nothing less than a nightmare.

Since this is my Hail Mary hoping to soften the hard hearts of the long-term board members, I am compelled to continue:

Can any of the following apply?

Malfeasance in office, or official misconduct, is the commission of an unlawful act, done in an official capacity, that affects the performance of official duties. Malfeasance in office is often grounds for a just cause removal of an elected official from office by state or recall election. (Recall unfortunately is not a PA option). Malfeasance in office contrasts with misfeasance in office, which is the commission of a lawful act, done in an official capacity, that improperly causes harm. Finally, nonfeasance in office is the abject failure to perform an official duty. Check out the lists above and you tell me.

What needs to Happen Now?

Some semblance of credibility needs to be restored for the board. Apparently, the Coughlin High School debacle of losing $6 million taxpayer's dollars is about to add another $1.2 million taxpayer's loss by selling the property for $1.8 million. The back story of the oldest high school in the state, of historic proportions is a monument to mismanagement. Pending mismanagement would be Elmer L. Meyers High school. Six-years ago, for a school in reasonably repairable state to last forever, the board's estimate for a demolition was $13 million. Today that would be $15 million, to destroy an architecturally significant, historic neighborhood cornerstone, leaving an empty lot worth a half million?

In November 2020 the City of Wilkes-Barre's City Council made the headlines with their ordinance to save historic buildings in the city:

HISTORY: Wilkes-Barre ordinance exception to the norm in Pa.

Subheading: Saving History, one building at a time. I [Richard Holodick] responded to the article.

Public Schools Form an Essential Part of Pennsylvania's Architectural Heritage

A feature article, "Saving History One Building at a Time." No mention of the state's oldest high school, Coughlin; no mention of GAR high school labeled the most beautiful; no mention of historic, architectural significant Elemer L. Meyers High School. Second headline, "HISTORY: Wilkes-Barre ordinance exception to the norm in Pa." The exception to the norm is the WBA school board who is not destroying one historic building, they have been meticulously, slowly destroying over the years three historic schools. City council to their credit has made giant steps to preserve our city's treasures; to their discredit, ignored our three magnificent high schools; doubling down they will leave the city without a high school. Hopefully the newly created Historic District Advisory Committee will "deem the three high schools historic.

When considering the amount of money that can be saved by restoring the historic facilities and the documented fact that the schools will have a forever shelf life, what has taken place is unconscionable and irresponsible! Mr. Caffery, board president, has stated the need for this board to have a "Legacy." The destruction of this once nationally recognized school will come in second to placing public school children on a coal ash toxic, subsidence -prone dump. The board needs three action items: The first is a motion for Bancroft Inc. or an equally qualified restoration firm to provide a second opinion on MHS. The other two are below the charts.

The West Shore School District

There are places advertised on the Internet such as The West Shore School District where a Superintendent and Board can go to make WBA a better school district. Why not?

WBA needs to conduct this survey! Phasing to control costs.

West Shore: "Building on a Tradition of Excellence." They care about their children, the community and taxpayers. WBA needs to care also.

The second motion to conduct a district wide survey comparable to the West Shore School District, or the Centre County School District survey; taxpayers, because they must pay for it, faculty and staff, because they must live with it.

The third action item is an RFP to solicit bids to conduct a search for a qualified firm to do a long-range curriculum/facility master plan. The purpose is to identify activities that will improve the dismal academic scoring, and to specifically address six other neglected facilities, that will be considerably restrained by the astronomical debt incurred for the consolidation for only 2400 students, leaving 4600 students in need of facility improvements/replacement. These three actions items will go a long way to bringing credibility to this board.

The Pa. Department of Education, Pa. School boards Association, the American Institute of Architects, & the Pa. Historical Society, and most of the board members & the community, support neighborhood schools. So what does our board do? It closes neighborhood schools! To save money? That ship has sailed, as our neighboring districts have experienced. Consolidation does not save money. Our board already knew that when they decided to run the public through this misery.

My Recommendation: This sitting board cannot and should not accept responsibility for what has transpired in the past. However, they must learn from the past. Secondly, the district is in dire straits relating to student achievement, facilities (six lower-level schools), a building site best described as at risk, and an underfunded district facing a half billion dollars fix to right the district.

Yes, there is more. Add a devasting factor COVID 19, costing quality education, additional costs for teaching supplies for hybrid instruction, bussing, and the potential loss of students fleeing the district to charter and cyber schools now being experienced by our surrounding districts.

What happens when the new school is under enrolled, even 25% coupled with students leaving to go to charter or cyber schools. Will the district have problems meeting its debt service. Enough said! This board—in fact any board and administration cannot do it alone. Sports junkies know that there is no I in team. So what should WBASD do? Is there any hope?.

The first and most vital step is the long-range curriculum/facility master plan that begins as early as possible 20/21. Then the board must execute a complete reversal of utilizing existing resources and external advice/research. It has not worked.

Additional advice comes in the form of a recommendation to change: Put aside any thoughts of

"If we build it they will come."

The board needs to know now, will the parents, guardians, uncles and aunts send their children to the new school? The board needs to know from those who walk the walk, teachers, administrators, support staff and custodians/maintenance personnel.

Their opinions on this project and what needs to be done on the academic side are vital. The board need to hear from those who must pay for the project and the operational budgets to support the newly configured school district.

The West Shore School District's survey accomplishes all that and more. More being credibility with the community. The past five years has been a discrediting of the soundness/safety of Meyers High School. It's up for sale, information is needed as its stability and verifiable uses.

The board has in hand a proposal from an award-winning large school restoration firm who will provide a second opinion on the historic facility at a cost under $100,000. If we can pay $86,000 to move practice fields, a million to fast track, a million to expand an un-needed swimming pool we can afford this study. The fact is as I have shown in this brief treatise, we cannot afford not to do it.

The ball is in your court with ahem, five basketball coaches on this board. Perhaps contract with wo-Time Superintendent of the Year and Lifelong Educator, Dr. Terry Grier.

Dr. Grier

Thank you for your time. After you digest this report, feel free to contact me and I would be happy to meet with you at your convenience

Sincerely

Richard A. Holodick, Ph.D.

Chapter 1 Introduction to Issues re WBA School Board

There are no qualifications to be on a public-school board, and no compensation. The time commitment is substantial, the magnitude of responsibility is overwhelming. Criticism is abundant. The operative question: Is there a better way to govern public school?

The following chapters can best be described as a "Statement of the Problems," and a protocol for corrective action. Bold would describe the actions that are recommended. Considering this, the credibility of this book and chapter author (Richard Holodick) is needed. The following will illustrate my education and experience, but also my biases as to the areas of my concentration throughout my career.

I was born with a physical handicap, included a speech impediment which may have contributed to early academic deficiencies in 1st through 12th grade. But let me tell you this. It did give me tougher skin. The picture of Mom and I above was taken in 1938. Mom was in the first graduating class ever at Meyers High. Both sides of a 1937 post card are pictured below. The fourth picture is Dr. Thomas Payzant, a Harvard Ph.D. former US Assistant Secretary of Education, I was his assistant superintendent OKC.

ELMER MEYERS HIGH SCHOOL, WILKES-BARRE, PA.

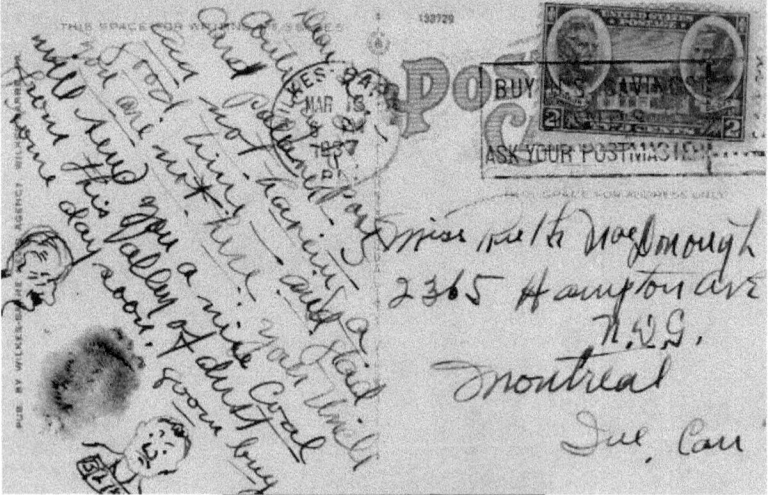

Dr. Thomas Payzant

Counselors once cautioned me: "Richard you will never be a radio announcer, or a college graduate, look to the trades." That turned out to be a motivator for me. After a little less than a dozen years later, I worked as an International Brotherhood of Electrical Workers electrician. Great job! That evolved into my first a teaching position.

I found myself teaching adults at a tech school. It required that I finish some part-time college courses where I soon discovered that I was not as stupid as I was told. I quickly updated the press clippings in my mind. I was unstoppable. Soon it seemed, I had my B.S. degree in education; then a master's in administration. This success led to a national scholarship by the US Department of Education by which I was able to earn a Ph.D.

I did not have a dime and that was good because not a dime of my own was needed—not even for books or housing. This completed my goal of earning degrees from three universities, Temple, Penn State, and Colorado State. I had an early goal to work at the secondary, community college, and university levels.

The secondary experience was at a K-12 metro school district, 5000 employees, 42,000 students; we bussed 12,000 students. The community College experience was as an associate dean at Aims Community College, Greeley Colorado. Also, at the community college level was as Director of Planning City Colleges of Chicago, one of the largest systems in the nation serving 77,000 students a year in nine facilities. University level, I was a full-time employee at Penn State, main campus with classmates Franko Harris and Jimmy Cefalo.

I am especially proud of the fact that both the Oklahoma and Chicago employments were conducted on a nationwide search. The superintendent selecting me was an US Assistant Secretary of Education. My assignment as assistant superintendent in OKC, was to create a new school district working with the Honorable George Nigh, Governor, and a three-star US Air Force retired General, (McNickle) commander of the Tinker Air force base in Moore Oklahoma. Also, a corporate attorney, she served on the board for 32 years.

In Williamsport Pa. I created, developed and supervised a 600-student school without walls. There was a German style apprenticeship program for the at-risk students, academic underachievers that turned these students around to a point of having Peter Jennings news program give the students five minutes of national coverage. Also, two students were given awards in the Rose Garden by President Clinton.

For 20 years. I engaged as a part time consulting for an international facility master planning firm. My education and experience were in four states, requiring 27 moves. My son Robert understandably thought his last name was U-Haul.

I assisted locally in the writing of educational and equipment specifications for the Luzerne County Community College, Misericordia University nursing program, and the Perry Traditional Academy in Pittsburg. I was then contracted by the Pa. Department of Education to do an articulation agreement between Pittsburg University, the Allegheny Community College, the catholic high schools and four area vocational-technical schools. Additionally, through the PDE I had the distinction of conducting an articulation agreement between LCCC and the West Side Vocational-Technical School.

My skills include part time private & public school involvement with places such as Hewitt Packard, Villanova University, Kodak of Colorado, and Millersville College.

In this book, please know that I used all of the capabilities that I gained over the years leading up to the present time. I am pleased to tell the book reader why my substantial experience in education gave me the proper background to engage in the analysis of the Wilkes-Barre Area School District and its governance.

I have the hope that you will learn about the actions taken by a democratically elected board of directors whose job it is to manage the affairs of the Wilkes-Barre Area School District on behalf of the students and the public. It is a shame that the district is seriously underfunded by the state but so are a lot of other school districts. The average salary of its residents is at the poverty level but the average salary of district personnel far exceeds that of the general public in WB Area.

You will learn that there are many senior citizens living on fixed incomes who cannot afford Taj Mahal schools and teachers who pull in fine salaries. I am not suggesting that we adjust salaries but it helps for the district employees to understand that life is not so good for the constituency.

Unfortunately, in this book and through other sources, you will also learn that though this board was duly elected by the people, they were misled about the board's intentions. In fact, the elected board misrepresented itself by agreeing, if elected, to represent the people and provide for the academic needs of the students above all else.

Were they kidding or were they inept? The story is too big to tell it all, but we do tell most of it in this two-volume book. We will cite quotations from citizens subject to the board's dictates. You will see that they have chosen to follow what can only be concluded to be a misguided course of action rather than follow the known wishes and affordability limits of the people of the area, which they serve.

Very basic protocols (master planning & impact studies) for the education of students and attention to finances and facilities have been ignored by the major officials in WB Area to meet what some consider hidden agendas. The people need to ask the board what are those secret agendas?

The essence of the issue in dispute is whether perfectly maintainable and well-built and historically relevant neighborhood school structures in the City of Wilkes-Barre should be abandoned, discarded, and torn down so that the board can build its idea of a Taj Mahal school. Ladies and gentlemen, this is not just a public school built over a coal mine that has been reclaimed. The mine has not been reclaimed as per state regulations. The better use for the site would be as a mine in which workers wore haz-mat suits go safely in every day to collect the ore.

We keep forgetting that this school, The Big Toxic School, has its unstable foundation built on top of a toxic mine dump, in a community outside the major city in the school district. Both of your authors are originally from this city and both attended WBA schools so we both know how important it is to have a safe school to attend.

Neither of us can comprehend that the officials in Wilkes-Barre City would permit the School district to move out of the city to a neighboring city/community. This unfortunately for a lot of people means that the abandonment of Wilkes-Barre City, the county seat, leaves 67% of the school population with no high schools from three. How is that fair? Why would WB residents want to attend?

The board has determined. Let me repeat. The **board** has determined that the City which makes up over 60% of the school district simply does not matter. The board expects that city officials and the taxpayers of the city, when this is properly explained to them will be willing to give up its high schools for this board's potentially hazardous folly. Perhaps Wilkes-Barre can use these buildings to recreate the Wilkes-Barre School District and secede from an organization that chooses not to be the caretaker of its best interests. Please do not let the board sell these buildings! They represent the next iteration of Wilkes-Barre High. We can do it.

For over 100 years, these three WB City High Schools have met the needs of the students and the taxpayers in City high schools named Coughlin, GAR, and Meyers. Why would the citizens of Wilkes-Barre enroll in a school out of town because a Superintendent from Mountaintop, not Wilkes-Barre said it had to be so. In America , who works for whom?

The Wilkes-Barre School District can also accept students from other communities. Let the Wilkes-Barre School Board eat their Taj Mahal Big Toxic School.

The current board has not served its constituents well and has shut the public out of the major decision making. They began a half billion-dollar building project (construction renovations) with no curriculum/facility master plan. They still have no maintenance plan for the new school and have had no plan for the upkeep of school buildings for over fifty years if ever.

They have no qualified staff to provide maintenance work in any of the $300,000,000 worth of properties, which are "owned" by the school district. Why is this so important? If the board had the proper team of in-house builders, and maintainers, and a plan for them to do their jobs regularly keeping the properties maintained, there would not be an "urgent" need today to replace the three historically relevant high schools in Wilkes-Barre City with an abomination built outside the city limits on top of a toxic mine shaft.

The board, over the citizens objections, plans to tear down these historical structures because as trustees of district property, they exercised a one-word board maintenance philosophy of neglect, neglect, and neglect, repeated three times for effect.

Just something to whet your appetite!

This is a school district supporting that are within 124 square miles. There are in fact, many pristine locations. Only seven have been selected to be considered. There are only three sites of the seven examined that were not owned by the district—Pagnotti (current site), Biscontini, and the Murray sites.

What was the first choice? The only district-owned site that forbade public schools by zoning regs. It was just 2.7-acres in size. The state of PA as well as common sense recommends at least 35 acres for a new school. The board decision was all packaged in a plan that segregated the high school with the largest percentage of minority students. Dr. Richard Holodick met with the superintendent, solicitor, and facilities committee warning them that a zoning failure could happen.

There were twenty- seven people, including attorney Kim Borland, a 20- year district volunteer, who begged the board to table this action. They went ahead despite the opposing advice. They did not succeed in their zoning request. The zoning failure cost the taxpayers $6 million.

One would logically think that after getting burnt, more thought would prevail in selecting the next site. But it did not. The board rejected many pleas from those who suggested that the Murry parcel would be ideal. Again the board disagreed making the public statement with the statement that the site was near a busy street and next to railroad tracks, therefore "unsafe."

Ironically, they picked the least safe of any site possible—a site mocked because of its toxicity. This site would be rejected immediately because of the toxic terrain by 5 other states. It is next to the Cross Valley Expressway, near railroad tracks, isolated from neighborhoods, (prisons are isolated from neighborhoods) the site is "subsidence prone." The land was a strip/deep mined, unlined coal ash dump, an industrial waste dump. And, despite all that, the board found it safer than the pristine Murray site.

Looking at where the board conducts its meetings, this picture above shows that this can be best described as an arrogance configuration, befitting this board and nobody else. This is a large school cafeteria where the dais could be straight, but the board dais is in a horseshoe shape. It means that part of the board members on both sides will have their backs to their constituents, students and staff attending the meeting.

For the hearing impaired who rely on lip reading, yours truly, it is near impossible to hear what is going on—an apparent board preference. There are nine board members, a board secretary, a solicitor, a business manager, and the superintendent--normally 12 people on the dais.

This district has a $121 million operating budget, has a quarter of a billion-dollar construction project on going, paid a million to" RUSH" the project, a million to expand the swimming pool, and $83,000 to move the practice fields, and one microphone for 12 people. This is the best they could do for a board meeting.

A person making $500 taxpayer's dollar a day gets up to pass the microphone to the person speaking. I attended a district basketball game and counted 60 basketballs, only one is needed for the game. There are five basketball coaches on the WBA board but I'm getting silly: right?

May I point out that on June 15, 2015, I attended the most disgraceful, unprofessional, saddest, dysfunctional, illegal board meeting in, my 50 years attending board meetings; with seventeen years sitting on the dais. It was the purpose of this "rushed" board meeting to get a proposal to PDE, Plan Con Division before July 1st.

The hurried plan was to consolidate Coughlin & Meyers high schools on a site, 2.7 acres, that forbid public high schools. A speaker at the zoning hearing said it was like trying to put a size sixteen foot in a size four shoe. But the board chose to do it anyway and failed.

Chapter 2 A Recalcitrant School Board

The board failed and they are preparing to fail again. The board's dream school should not be built because the old is better than the new. Well-built forever schools should not be replaced. It is difficult to understand building new when major agencies have published that schools should *renovate*. Notably, those on the renovate side include **The Pennsylvania Department of Education and the Pa. School Boards Association. These are the WBA school district's advisors. Additionally, the Pa. Historical Society supports renovations.**

A major city (Wilkes-Barre, PA) will face neighborhood blight by removing three major reasons for people to live there. Despite grave warnings of children and staff potentially getting sick on toxic waste from the new school site, this board has chosen to place the health of students at risk.

Please tell me what esteemed body working for the public good would subject those learning or working at Mine Shaft High. from the toxic material, water, and fumes from the designed school built on top of a hazardous waste dump. It is unconscionable.

The board says that it is relying on the claims of the DEP that the dangerous chemicals can be capped. Five states forbid building near a contaminated site; 29 others have very strict regulations for concern of the children. Is the WBASB a leader in toxic prevention or does it have an agenda reason to reject the prudent actions of other states?

More and more citizens of the Area believe the public was duped into believing the words of the consigliere that putting poverty level Wilkes-Barre Area citizens in debt up to a half billion or more dollars after the State's contribution, was the only solution to having children well-educated in this area. Soon the foreclosure teams from the county and other taxing bodies will be coming for all the properties of the elderly who will not be able to pay the taxes required for the board's Taj Mahal. Citizens of WB Area, there is no need for this monstrosity.

The board was provided restoration costs by firms with zero large school restoration experience. As expected by the public, with the spirit of collegiality among the contractors, as expected, the bids were highly inflated. They included sizing for earthquake protection, in Northeast Pa? Most homeowners and businesses in the area pretty much ignore the option of earthquake coverage when they buy an insurance policy. After all, they reasoned, it's not as if we live in California.

The restoration of architecturally significant and historic high schools when done correctly creates a forever shelf life for the structures. There is no way to estimate the cost savings but for sure it would not be the $ half billion over 40 years for the Big Toxic School. The private sector loves to buy abandoned WBASD schools because they are so well built. What do they know?

The following, such as Guthrie School – now owned by Metro, is just one former WBA school, renovated by the private sector. Pictures of others are below. Ironically, one of the district's architect firms is in this forever shelf-life building, right up the street from toxic high.

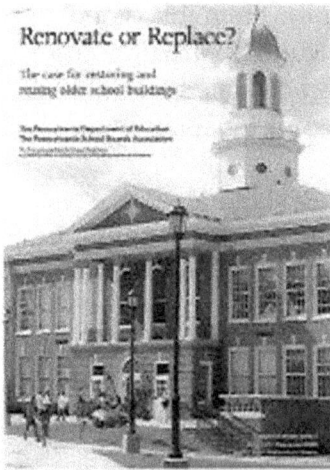

We show a few examples of the school district's discarded school buildings. The first is the Guthrie School, corporate headquarters for Metro. This facility has been restored and is energy efficient. Because of its age it will have a forever shelf life.

This former school is now a corporate center, this structure will also have a forever shelf life, it is the home for one of the school district's architectural firms.

Please refer to the five pictures in the ribbon on the prior page. Comparing "Infamous" to WBASB Corruption, raising the question;

is this the best we can do governing school districts? This is the story about a group of people who swore a public oath and ignored it. The title of this book could very well be The Bad School Board. When you finish this book, I predict you will be convinced when they did their worst deeds against the students, community, and taxpayers, in a word, their decisions were bad.

In a community's struggle for safe, enduring, neighborhood schools you will learn the sordid details of Wilkes-Barre Area's corruption, deception, back-breaking taxation, and yes, even tyranny against the people. It is a story worth telling. It may not be the worst story of corruption you have ever been told but it is bad, bad, bad. You may even say that the stories leading up to the Wilkes-Barre Area School Board's Big Toxic School beats a lot of other stories such as Bad Education, Kids for Cash, and Erin Brockovich.

Admittedly, no children have died yet as in the pollution of Hicksville in Erin Brockovich, but the future predictions may make Brockovich's story seem like small potatoes, considering serious health issues and potential subsidence at the Big Toxic School.

Luzerne county was the home of Russel Bufalino, a mafia crime leader featured in the film "The Irishman." Each of these four stories are bad and after you read our story of WBASB in this book, you may agree it almost tops the three cited. To get you thinking of corruption and graft regarding the Wilkes-Barre School Board, please permit me to cite a few further exposes on the model politicians who have served on the Wilkes-Barre Area School Board.

Here is one from "gort42," a local, quite famous Pennsylvania blogger: Back in 2012, a blogger, who is known in NEPA as gort42 wrote a political commentary about the WBASB. Board Presidents from around that time were Pizzella and Elmy and there were a few bad guys on the board known as Dunn from the Dunn Deal and another President, Jim Height.

The Gort42 blogger pulled no punches about the board corruption. This is a sample of what the people think of the corrupt school board. The low opinion has prevailed for years and with good reason.

FRIDAY, DECEMBER 7, 2012
The State mandated re-organization meeting of the Wilkes-Barre Area School Board was held.

The reorganization meeting of the WBASB was anything but organized according to the story by Peter Cameron in the Citizens Voice with 2 breaks for executive sessions and Christine Katsock calling the meeting illegal via the Pa. Sunshine Act.

Former Coughlin HS teacher and sports coach John Quinn was elected President and Louis Elmy as VP. [Maybe nobody on the board is clean because of paternalism and cronyism and favoritism,] There are board members that didn't do "bad things", but silence is compliance.

You must wonder who would even want the job of school director in Wilkes-Barre. It does not pay anything, and you get a lot of grief in the local papers after you hire a relative for a position. Or maybe that's it. Maybe that is pay enough because nobody else gets that pay.

This is a body that has seen 3 members convicted of corruption. Jim Height, Brian Dunn and Frank Pizzella. After Pizzella was indicted he was elected as board President with the support of former reformer board member Christine Katsock.

If there is any government body in Luzerne County that needs to change its public persona it is this one (WBA board) but that doesn't seem to faze this bunch much. They made a hash of hiring a new superintendent and the new hiring policy is a joke. [They hired a novice for top dollar—his dad had been a former board member, father-in-law a state representative.]

Four seats are up in the upcoming election in May 2013. The incumbents are Christine Katsock, Lynn Evans, Phil Latinski and Bob Corcoran. I haven't heard if any of them will seek reelection.

Katsock ran for many offices as a Republican reformer before she finally got a spot on the school board. She came within 800 votes of defeating Wilkes-Barre Mayor Tom Leighton in 2003 and she gave State Rep Eddie Day Pashinski a run for his money in 2006. [She understands voting levers.]

She switched to the Democrats when she ran for the board and had no comment when asked to explain her vote for Pizzella but it's not hard to figure out if you look at her Campaign Finance Report. Frank Pizzella was her top cash contributor pitching in $3000. She also got $1800 as an in-kind contribution from the Friends of Frank Pizzella. Evans voted against Pizzella and the new super and revealed the pick system of filling jobs. Latinski goes along.

Bob Corcoran has other troubles. Update: Corcoran barred from home contact with son

Pure Bunkum has a couple of insightful posts about this subject such as getting rid of school boards. In fact, Keystone Politics proposes putting the Intermediate Units in charge.

Folks, please remember that there were four members (3 presidents) of the WBASB who faced political corruption charges over the years. It's tough to grab all their names at once but here they are:

Former Board Presidents

May 18, 2009 Jim Height, Sept 15, 2009 Frank Pizzella, Apr 7, 2016 Lou Elmy, Oct 7, 2010 Brian Dunn 2009. A New Year's Day wish for the Wilkes-Barre Area School Board (WBASB) at one point could have been to have no School board Presidents or members indicted in the following year.

Now, with the potential for additional discovered corruption in the Big Toxic School consolidation project (soon to be a scandal), the 2021 wish list may very well be a wish not to have all six members who voted for "Big Toxic," including the president, possibly indicted for fraud on the project. Few who are paying attention would be surprised if it came to that.

We are examining the multitude of errors and omissions by this board, factor in the fact that the only requirement to be on the board is residency. The public won't believe that you don't even need a high school diploma to be a board member. Yet this board is well degreed. We conclude in this book that election success is dependent on popularity, connections, and wallet size, and this raises even more questions:

Is this the best method of governing our school districts across the state if not the nation? Terry Grier nationally recognized change agent states, "If you don't have a great school board, you're not going to have a great school district.

There are problems in the WBASD, and they have been here for some time. The following is a Facebook post with some alterations from the author (Dr. Richard Holodick): Pay attention as these things just don't happen when there is good management at the central office and the board is holding people/agencies accountable.

The district's student's academic rank statewide is 443rd out of 500 school districts. WBASD has the most students in the state (600+) to flee to charter and cyber schools; with the largest number of truancies in the state; so those that do not flee stay home. 77% of the students are improvised (& parents).

Is this the Board's plan? That the District should consolidate sports, thereby meeting the goal of a 6A rank to play at the top level of sports in the state of PA. The board would like to close the three City-based high schools and consolidate them into one school. The school they picked to build is to be fashioned on an isolated site taking the 35% bussing of students (today's rate of bussers v walkers) to 95% of the students bussed; at $55,000+ a bus. There are no bargains at The Big Toxic School.

The WBA board all agree neighborhood schools are best but all of a sudden they began to profess openly that they cannot afford the three high schools. To supposedly save the taxpayers money they want to close neighborhood schools, move them out of the city, reduce varsity sports and extra curricula activities by two thirds.

The new school's location makes parent participation at the school impossible for many. This would be considered irresponsible because not only is the scholarly research opposed to such decisions, the district's own internal and external task force analyses by their own committees, as well as the community think tank known as Save Our Schools, Inc.

And the WBASB's own district funded facility feasibly study and the PFM state sponsored fiscal study lists such decisions as a disadvantage. That is a bit of an understatement.

How about building a new school? The PA. Department of Education, The Pa. School Boards Association, the American Institute of Architects, and the Pa. Historical Society, published, in favor of restoration vs building a new school. Yet, the board chose to build a new school. Why?

Please note: At a board meeting the board was informed that the library in the new school was too small to hold the recommended volumes. Nonetheless, this was ignored. At the very next board meeting, instead of addressing the library quandary, the board voted to expand the swimming pool two more lanes and improve the school flooring at a cost of a million dollars. The reason for the added lanes was to qualify hosting competitive events. Due to soil conditions (subsidence), a deep diving pool was not possible, negating any completive events at Toxic High. The district now has an eight lane Olympic size pool to teach senior high students to swim. Problem is; they already had one.

It should be noted that this poverty level underfunded district has a swimming pool, with a diving pool, in an elementary school where students need to learn to swim. Same scenario with the planned football stadium at Toxic High; the district already has a great football stadium. Of course, a new pool and football stadium would be nice, but we can't afford it!

The consolidated school is already being constructed on a strip mined, deep mined, coal ash dump, former industrial waste dump, with the state cautionary that the site has a history of subsidence. What can make such a site work other than nothing?

GUEST COMMENTARY

Alternate school plan keeps neighborhood concept in place

Richard A Holodick's Face Book post. Holodick has gathered stats taken from 2014, that may be even higher at this point. Academically all students do better in neighborhood schools, yes even the gifted. Yet, the Board's plan is to close the three neighborhood schools.

In the new consolidated school, these students will need parent or guardian help, near impossible for some once we isolate their school.

The Board chooses to ignore the fact that this is a poverty level district and acts like the district has unlimited funds. This new project they have entered will cost residents that earn an average of $38,000 a year a half billion dollars over a forty-year period. This is most discouraging as it satisfies the facility need for only a third of the students (2400). This leaves the improvised children (4600) wanting and five aged elementary schools to accommodate the bulk of the students.

The consolidated WBASD High School PLAN Before Big Toxic High. The Wilkes-Barre Area School, WBASD district is comprised of 67,000 residents, 76% of them are at the poverty level with an average income of $38,000 a year. There are 7,000 students in seven neglected aged facilities, the district's # 2 problem.

Problem # 1 is student's failure with a rank of 443 out of 501 school districts in Pennsylvania. Some remember that just eight years ago with Dr. Jeffrey Namey at the helm, the district students were ranked 144th out of 500 school districts. In 1968 the WBA was academically ranked as one of the tops in the nation.

Problem # 3, experienced leadership at the central administrative office, and professional contracted services. The board is highly educated with four retired administrators, a degreed minister of color, but have been and continuing to be dysfunctional. The standard procedures of curriculum/facility long range planning have been ignored.

Expenditures of a half billion dollars over a forty- year period are being wagered on a school for only 2400 students, leaving 4600 in need. For such a huge cost, one could safely label this act as irresponsible. In a poverty level district, underfunded by $33 million (about the budget of a modest motion picture) a year, not doing due diligence to use existing facilities, swimming pool and football stadium, no less historic facilities with a potential forever shelf life could easily run the district into educational and financial bankruptcy.

On top of that, the development of a plan to submit to the Pa. Department of Education that segregated the high school with the highest percentage of minorities and economically disadvantaged students constituted malfeasance in a public office.

The first concrete plan to build a consolidated school for 2400 students was downtown on 2.7 acres. The state recommends 35 acres. Besides being an inadequately sized lot, the downtown site was on a one-way narrow street that was forbidden by zoning. Nonetheless, this board went full speed ahead as if they could override city restrictions. They chose to begin spending money on this project like as if it were going to be approved by zoning. It was not approved and the impatience by this board cost the taxpayers $6 million.

Why did the board spend $6 million without a zoning waiver? This board treats taxpayer dollars like the goose producing golden eggs. Instead of reevaluating its decisions, this board doubles down on poor decision making; it even ignores any semblance of an impact study.

For example, after this first try cost $6 million, it quickly sped forward with another poor decision. It selected a candidate location out of 124 square miles which was the worst isolated, toxic, subsidence prone building site possible. The folly does not improve when we add the newest project was the costliest to buy and prep for building. Moreover, as if WBASD had deep pockets, in a "Robinhood" gesture the poverty ridden residents paid Pagnotti Enterprise, $55,000 an acre for land assessed at $10,000 an acre. This was a vivid example of the poor being robbed to pay the rich.

We continually discuss in both of the two volumes in this two-book set that the current site has the potential of putting children and district employees in harm's way. The topper is that if the mineral rights are worthless (they've never been assessed) the taxpayers paid

$55,000 an acre for land that had been assessed at $10,000 an acre (worth the repeat).

Though the Board sees golden eggs, the people and the auditors continue to see an impoverished public being stretched beyond their limits to pay their taxes. They see no gold or a goose and there is no way the locals can afford the burden being imposed. The Save Our Schools Inc. organization members, and legal reps have written complaints to the PDE Secretary of Education, the Auditor General, the Attorney General, the Pa. Inspector General, the FBI, and the Luzerne County District Attorney.

The deaf ears seem to show that the prevailing thought on the area influences even the top people in authority as a toxic school is being quietly built while Nero fiddles. We don't have to do this to ourselves.

This communication was sent directly to the Luzerne County District Attorney, Stefanie Salavantis:

Memorandum:

To: The Honorable Stefanie Salavantis, District Attorney, Luzerne County
From: Richard A Holodick, PhD.
Re: Wilkes-Barre Area School District
Date: October 28, 2020

I request that your office asks the Attorney General, Josh Shapiro to investigate this school district. Negligence and poor use of public funds are evident from the 100 complaints, and the audit. The property purchase price for a high school construction site, $4.2 million dollars or $55,000 an acre, five times the maximum assessed value is seriously suspicious.

Thirty-three WBA taxpayers sent 100 complaints to the Auditor General requesting his attention to questionable expenditures relating to the district's (unplanned) costly building project(s). The original building plan frittered away $6 million dollars without zoning approval, which was ultimately denied.

This might be considered misfeasance in a public office. Also reported was the purchase of un-reclaimed mining land, when state law requires the owner to reclaim the land prior to the sale. In addition, the board authorized taxpayers to improve the land they did not own.

The results: Auditor General Eugene DePasquale has completed a review of the Wilkes-Barre Area School District's high school consolidation plan and commended the district for making "tough decisions" that will "generate cost savings." He did admit, " "Based on the limited scope of review, my team found the Wilkes-Barre Area School District is working to create a safe learning environment for students, faculty and staff," DePasquale said a statement released after his audit on a Wednesday. I say, Safe on a toxic dump? "AG commends Wilkes-Barre Area's consolidation plan."

When we review the state mandated 2016 audit, and it is stated in the audit that the district over spent the approved operational budget three years in a row, was a violation of Pa. School code 609. There is strong evidence that a combination of malfeasance and misfeasance may have occurred.

I request that the Attorney General make this determination one way or another—a response is requested as to what action, if any, was taken on the violation of State Code 609, for three consecutive years when substantial taxpayer dollars were lost?

Finally, I feel that there has been an erosion of public trust by this board of education.

To: Board membership January 2014
President Louis Elmy, Joe Caffery, Ned Evans, Nino Galella, Christine Katsock, John Quinn, David Susek, Denise Thomas, and Rev. Shawn Walker.

cc: Inspector General, Attorney General, Auditor General

Chapter 3 A New Broom Sweeps Clean

Bring on the new broom

Nationally prominent author Brian Kelly, a co-author of this two-book set, wrote his 202nd book on August 11, 2019. You may know that Brian is the most published living non-fiction author in the United States. His 2019 book is a tell-all tale about the Wilkes-Barre Area School Board. Yes, folks, it was tough to find enough paper to print all the pages he produced.

The Big Toxic School!

Wilkes-Barre Area's Tale of Corruption, Deception, Taxation & Tyranny

A struggle for safe, enduring neighborhood schools.

By Brian W. Kelly

We can't wait until there are no WB high schools & the tax burden is unsustainable.

Rendering of Mine Shaft High

A purpose of the book at the time in 2019, was to help the people of the area elect an honest school board. Election day was set for Nov 5, 2019. If the board could not be swept clean, it was hoped that the public would at least embarrass the school board to call off its plans to build an unaffordable multi-million-dollar new high school on top of a toxic mine dump.

Dr. Richard A. Holodick, President of Save Our Schools is best portrayed by the following Letter to the Editor. Richard Holodick states, beating this school board has always been the best way to bring honest governance back to a board that had gone south on the people.

As the president of Save Our Schools, an advocacy group he formed with others to fight the school board's tyranny, Holodick had signed off on a subtitle for The Big Toxic School as follows. He saw his battle as "Wilkes-Barre Area's four-pronged tale of 1. Corruption, 2. Deception, 3. Taxation & 4. Tyranny." For Holodick and the Save our Schools group, it had been a long tough battle with more downs than ups in engaging a board that would not fight fairly.

In fact, the board thinks it has won the war as the Big Toxic School is in the process of being built on a mountain in Plains Twp. Meanwhile, Wilkes-Barre, with its three high schools teetering in the balance, is the biggest city in the area is to be left with no high schools. Save our Schools and its President Richard Holodick have not given up the fight. There is still much war to raise and this second book about our plight and our just deserve to win is going to position us for a victory march.

Dr. Holodick, who the school board views as a nemesis though he sees himself as an ally for the people adds "The news media has suggested that SOS back off the opposition and support the new school as it is now nearly half complete. If the issue was that the consolidation was academically stupid, and the project thus far in the construction phase, SOS would "stand down."

However, three is no denying that The Big Toxic School is built on a very toxic site, subsidence prone, and the district is depending on the DEP to ensure the safety of our children. This is the agency presently under investigation by a PA Grand Jury for not monitoring the fracking industry properly. It is a downright scary scenario when the Attorney General publicly states that it appears that DEP monitoring is dependent on the size of the wallet or the connections with the elite power brokers.

Five other states have offered their truth v the WBASB preached falsehoods. To protect the school children, they forbid building a public school NEAR a contaminated site. Twenty-nine other have regulations so strict a public school could not be built on the Pagnotti site. What is wrong with Pennsylvania Official's?

The WBASB build a school directly on top of a contaminated site. No public school has ever been built on a site with this many draw backs. No school district has paid five times the lowest assessed value for a dump. Surely there is corruption involved. Can there be no investigations at the state level or federal level because there are some favorites who might get upset?

The Save our Schools (SOS) Group is the major opponent of the construction of a new $121 million high school in Plains Township. With all other expenses, local taxpayers fear a $ half billion-dollar tab over 40 years. On election day the group began with strong odds that SOS would find at least two new members sympathetic to their cause to be on the board this past December, 2019. That did happen but SOS needed two more victors to gain a majority.

| Debra Formola | Jody Busch | Terry Schiowitz | Robin Shudak | Beth Anne Owens-Harris |

Two write-in candidates, Jody Bush and Debra Formola, if elected in a long shot would have given SOS a 5-4 board majority but write-ins are tough to win in Pennsylvania. We'll win next year when Jody and Debra are able to run as full party candidates. It should be noted that Busch and Formola broke all records with the number of write in votes they did garner.

Robin Shudak withdrew from the ballot. Former district school psychologist Beth Ann Owens-Harris got the most votes in this election with 5,062, while Terry Schiowitz was third with 4,784. All three incumbents who had supported the building of the Big Toxic School were reelected.

Along with Rev. Shawn Walker, Mark Atherton came in second and John Quinn came in fourth. Walker ran only on the Democratic ticket. SOS is convinced that because of the corruption, deception, future unaffordable taxation, and the tyranny of the board against the people, they can stop the building project before the next election and protect the taxpayers from fiscal and educational bankruptcy.

The group is seeking help from the PA Auditor General, the Attorney General, and the U.S. Department of the Interior who is looking into the Pa. DEP. There are many sides of the project activity so far that do not pass the smell test. We will tell you about those in this book. Brian W. Kelly, Author of 259 non-fiction books, #1 in the US, has joined Dr. Holodick in this effort to tell the people that it is not too late.

Taking on the Bad Guys in Wilkes-Barre

Brian Kelly has often written about his co-author, the gristly Richard Holodick. Kelly says that Holodick is a never-say-die leader who was encouraged by the success of Erin Brockovich in taking on the big guys in a chemical case and winning. Holodick thinks that the people of the Wilkes-Barre Area in Pennsylvania can also beat the big guys with all their political connections even though the area is still fraught with the same level of nepotism and cronyism—still rampant despite the famous kids for cash convictions.

It appears clear that earlier boards did not fear the FBI when they charged a board member and the board went ahead despite the charges and elected him president of the board even after the indictment. It appears that bad behavior such as racist beliefs, posted on Face Book, or the member's level of education / experience did not matter as former school clerk Denise Thomas was elected president and most recently vice president.

The first comment by her sister and she agreed "even better," regarding Mexicans and Methodists. In a second post, an in-depth evaluation by a clerk? Not becoming any adult let alone a public-school director. There were e-mail posts from her computer that led to a news media headline, "2nd WBA school board member in hot water."

The WBA School Board's Credibility

We now turn to a nationally known public education reformer, one of the best in the country.

Two-Time Superintendent of the Year and Lifelong Educator, Dr. Terry Grier, is known for his saying: "If you don't have a great school board, you're not going to have a great school district." This reflects Grier's opinion that not only is board leadership important but the superintendent, building principals and teachers are vital to the success of a school district.

Grier touts a groundbreaking formula that he used to improve the seventh largest district in the country and earn national recognition as a reformer." Leadership, rigor, accountability, choice and community engagement are reoccurring themes for this outstanding school reformer. Does our Governing Board meet the Grier standard? Not hardly!

The Board's past credibility was clearly marred by FBI indictments, and the imprisonment of three board members and a district employee. The indictments were for board member's "pay to play" activities, having teachers, administrators, support personal and vendors pay for their jobs and their opportunity to provide fee services.

Board Members Don't Plan To Fail

They Failed To Plan A Curriculm/Facility Long Range Master Plan

Board credibility was further damaged by rampant nepotism and cronyism. The word on the street was that many family trees grow and are growing within the WBA school district. Most notable, and somewhat humorous was a taxpayer insisting on a reduction in the number of staff who are related. Ned Evans (of course) a board member blurted out at a meeting "sure you try sitting here and voting your wife out."

There were four board member's wives working for the district at that time. The other three looked like the deer in the head lights. Such honesty was not expected.

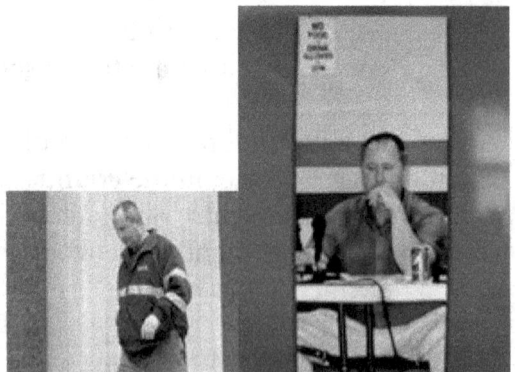

Former W-B Area board president
faces life in prison

WILKES-BARRE — Louis Elmy, former president of the Wilkes-Barre Area School Board, will plead guilty to federal extortion and weapons charges that could send him to prison for life, according to the U.S. Department of Justice.

Elmy, of Wilkes-Barre, was charged in February with drug trafficking and a felony weapons offense. He reached an agreement with federal prosecutors on a plea deal this week, the Justice Department announced Thursday.

The charges against Elmy stem from his alleged actions while employed as a counselor in the work release program at Luzerne County Correctional Facility, according to the Justice Department.

Louis Elmy, when leaving Federal Court, Scranton Pa. where he faced a possible life in prison wished it was all behind him. Then Board President Elmy, broke school district law in small things such as no beverages allowed in the gym (sign on wall behind him), while he had a Pepsi sitting in front of him. Arrogance? Yes! But the FBI's charge of extortion was the topper.

A half dozen years back the board president faced a life sentence for extortion, forging the signatures of three sitting judges, drugs, weapon possession without a permit to carry. Although not related to the school district, during his tenure on the board as president the district over spent the operating budget for three years with a high of $10,000—state violation Code 609. This is bad, bad, but it's gets worse!

Over a 50-year career, I have observed attending many board meetings, I have sat on the dais 17 years as a board CEO; and I have made public presentations to the boards of education at various locations. The present sitting board, which is a repeat board with the exception of Harris, Schiowitz and Patla, is not expected to make any new overtures to save their tenure. The public awaits the three new members to step forward to make the changes since silence is compliance. First of course they must overcome being in awe of their new peers. Of course, they are in the minority, but a motion to require a curriculum/facility master plan, would get a lot of attention.

There is a lot of needed board action for the record.

A motion to get a second opinion on the historic Meyers High School might fail with the intransigent majority on the board but it would be on the record. Dr. Holodick suggests that it is his opinion that the long-serving members of the board constitute the worst, uncaring, disorganized, and dysfunctional board majority that he has ever seen.

This group has heartlessly failed on so many levels. First, we look at the functionality of the board, policy and procedures manual—there is none. Conducting meetings or executing procedures, there is no reliance on Roberts Rules of Order—none!

Board agendas are delivered to board members the Friday before the Monday meeting; considering millions upon millions of items to pay it is not enough time to thoroughly review. The public receives the agenda the Sunday before the Monday meeting. Same problem.

The following were questionable inclusions for this book, but it does establish a board problem on several fronts, decency for starters, racism, morality, and seven other member's accountabilities.

Yes, by a unanimous vote, Board member Evans was asked to resign, but by law as an elected official he could not be forced to leave. But he was put on a committee and chaired one; why? A major charge for Thomas was the dozen raciest e-mails that came from her computer at GAR High School, where she was employed as a first level clerk. Her defense was that someone else typed and sent them while she was on break. The problem with her sister's post degrading Mexicans and Methodists was that the board member posted in agreement. Other social media questionable posts shed doubt on her claim someone else sent the derogatory posts from her computer. But in her own words on social media, *"I don't give a crap."*

The apology by former WBA teacher/administrator, (Evans) was for a post where he found humor in an Arizona teacher having oral sex with a student (I hope she didn't lose any teeth). The apology declined as It led to a first in the 100-year district history, eight board members, superintendent, and the NAACP requesting a board member's resignation. His response, I won't go!

Patla was joined by Harris and Schiowitz in the last election. She has not ever gone along to get along, standing her ground on the opposition to closing the neighborhood schools with a flawed educational and costly building plan. She refused the shovel and didn't wear the hard hat at the groundbreaking ceremony. It is obvious that she weathers being ostracized (cold water); will they climb the ladder or do what one former reformer said, "I go along to get along." Why do people operate they do? Often the reason is because things were always done that way.

Ned Evans
1 hr ·

I owe my CONSTITUANTS & FB FRIENDS the TRUTH. I was having a private convo with a friend after he posted a post. I made a lewd & totally unacceptable comment in which I posted my apologies for as an elected official afterwards & took down my comments.

Write a comment...

worked too hard on this Board & WILL NOT RESIGN much to the DISSATISFACTION OF THE SOS GROUP. That is " The TRUTH the whole TRUTH & nothing but the TRUTH so help me GOD. Thank you for hearing me out.

👍 Like   💬 Comment

Kris Conwell Jones and 24 others

Write a comment...

Ned Evans
I guess I'm a OLD WHITE MAN in this Congressman's eyes. IRONY. If I responded saying he was a young gay fag I would be inundated with remarks. This ass hole is a RACIST & should apologize to that woman he baggered.

Evans insists he won't go

Wilkes-Barre Area School Board Member Ned Evans is seen addressing NAACP President Guerline Laurore with his opinion during a school board meeting in April. Evans on Thursday said he will not resign in the wake of controversy over a social media post earlier this week.

See Patla picture on next page

l to r Ray Wendowloski, solicitor, Costello, Superintendent, Patla, Rev. Walker, Denise Thomas, board members. Patla was joined by Harris and Schiowitz in the last election.

The Monkey Ladder Experiment

There is something Dr. Holodick has experienced in several school districts. Board members campaign for school board seats with all the right reasons. With their good fortune, they get elected with the goal of making changes. Then, all of a sudden they become silent and begin to vote with the majority. There is a theory that fits what happens. Consider the new board member who says to himself or herself. "I go along to get along." When that fails maybe what follows becomes the reality of the day. OK, I admit that hosing may be extreme but ostracizing does happen and most humans can't take that. It is always easier to take the road more traveled. Going it alone has a lot of pitfalls.

- A group of scientists placed five monkeys in a cage, and in the middle, a ladder with bananas on top. Every time a monkey went up the ladder, the scientists soaked the rest of the monkeys with cold water.
- After a certain amount of this, each time a monkey would start up the ladder, the others would pull it down and beat that monkey; this too went on for a while. Eventually no monkey

would dare try climbing the ladder, no matter how great the temptation.

- The scientists then decided to replace one of the monkeys. The first thing this new monkey did, of course, was started to climb the ladder for the bananas. Immediately, the others pulled him down and beat him up.
- After several beatings, the new monkey learned never to go up the ladder, even though there was no evident reason not to— other than the severe beatings from peers.
- A second monkey entered the scenario and the same occurred. The first monkey participated in the beating of the second monkey. A third monkey was entered and the same was repeated. The fourth monkey was introduced, resulting in the same, before the fifth was finally replaced as well.
- What was left was a group of five monkeys that — without ever having received a cold shower — were prepared to beat up any monkey who attempted to climb the ladder.
- If it was possible to ask the monkeys why they beat up on all those who attempted to climb the ladder, their most likely answer would be "I don't know. It's just how things are done around here."

Does that sound at all familiar?

The most damaging phrase in the language is: 'It's always been done that way.' ~ Grace Hopper

Annoyance Factors

Actually, the following goes beyond being annoying. Remember there are four highly educated educators on this board who were trained to be aware of the needs of sight and hearing impaired. There are nine board members, the solicitor, and the business manager on the dais. The board most recently in a large cafeteria sit in a horseshoe arrangement, which has some members with their backs to the constituents or side view. It makes it difficult for both the sight and hearing impaired.

With an operating budget exceeding a hundred million dollars the board can only afford one microphone that is sometimes passed to the board member, solicitor, or business manager that is speaking. Normally board meetings are held on Mondays, board members receive their packets the Friday before. Millions of dollars in purchasing, construction change orders, a list of new hires with no names attached. Board actions on the millions is done with no discussion. New hires names are mentioned when they call for action.

A policy/procedure for board operation such as Robert's Rules of Order does not exist. Example, at the end of a meeting Rev. Walker made a motion to increase the student population 33% in the new school (800 students). Not in Friday's packet, not an agenda item, no costs were supplied, and the public did not have a chance to comment on a very costly action item. or even asked for, and the action passed.

How does a board approve the expenditure of tax dollars without knowing the amount? The following is the board action to buy the Pagnotti site; note "at the appraised value." Appraised value $10,000 an acre, board, no taxpayer's paid $55,000 an acre for a toxic contaminated subsidence prone dump.

It appears clear that the earlier board did not fear the FBI when they charged a board member and the board elected him president after the indictment." It appears that bad behavior such as racist beliefs, posted on Face Book, or level of education / experience matter because former school clerk Denise Thomas was elected president and most recently vice president. The first by her sister and she agreed "even better" regarding Mexicans and Methodists. Second post, an in-depth evaluation by a clerk? Not becoming any adult let alone a public-school director. There were e-mail posts from her computer that led to a news media headline, "2nd WBA school board member in hot water."

2nd WBA director in hot water

By Mark Guydish
mguydish@timesleader.com

WILKES-BARRE — Denise Thomas became the second Wilkes-Barre Area School Board member this week grappling with calls for her resignation thanks to Facebook posts.

Denise Thomas
Dec 28 at 4:34pm ·

My New Years resolution:

To be much more vocal and critical towards the inept, nay sayers and ANYONE who criticizes our school district, our employees and students without having a clue....

After all....
We could be in the same position as the Scranton and MANY other School Districts...
But we've had and continue to have the "audacity" not to be,...

Write a comment....

Denise's "New Year's Resolution," speaks volumes, putting down "anyone who criticizes our school district, our employees, and students without having a clue." When the "district" spends $6 million on a failed project; its students at the bottom academically statewide, and the very best site to place our children on is an unlined coal ash and industrial waste dump, subsidence prone, and we pay five times the assessed value, it is the board majority that is clueless.

We are not in the same position as Scranton, Denise is correct, placing our children on 78 acres of toxic/subsidence land is far worse than Scranton. This board cannot take criticism or give criticism through holding people agencies accountable.

🔊 **im·be·cile**

/ˈimbəsəl/

noun INFORMAL

1. a stupid person.

   synonyms: fool, idiot, cretin, moron, dolt, halfwit, ass, dunce, dullard, simpleton, nincompoop, blockhead, ignoramus, clod; *informal* dope, thickhead, ninny, chump, dimwit, dummy, dum-dum, dumbbell, jackass, bonehead, fathead, numbskull, dunderhead, airhead, pinhead, lamebrain, peabrain, birdbrain, dipstick, donkey, noodle; *informal* nit, nitwit, twit.

<   Denise's Post   •••

AnnMarie Petitto-Thomas
How about: rustlers, cut throats, murderers, bounty hunters, desperados, mugs, pugs, thugs, nitwits, halfwits, dimwits, vipers, snipers, con men, Indian agents, Mexican bandits, muggers, buggerers, bushwhackers, hornswogglers, horse thieves, bull dykes, train robbers, bank robbers, ass-kickers, shit-kickers and Methodists!

Like

Denise Thomas
AnnMarie Petitto-Thomas even better!!

Dr. Holodick received "im-be-cile" by the US postal service, no return address, no note, no name of sender. It's also posted on Face book. This post done by a WBA board member. Thomas claims the derogatory, 13 racist e-mails from her computer when she worked as a clerk for the district were not done by her, these Face Book posts question that.

The "kids for cash" scandal was a tough victory for the area yet, justice prevailed eventually. It centered on judicial kickbacks to two judges at the Luzerne County Court of Common Pleas in Wilkes-Barre, Pennsylvania. Here are the salient aspects of the case: Criminal verdicts and sentences, validation that there exists a "Culture of Corruption, "in this county. A judicial system gone awry, with a school district governance board as well. Both have affected the lives of our most precious resource, our children.

On February 18, 2011, following a trial, a federal jury convicted Ciavarella on 12 of the 39 remaining counts he faced including racketeering, a crime in which prosecutors said the former judge used children "as pawns to enrich himself." In convicting Ciavarella of racketeering, the jury agreed with prosecutors that he and Conahan had taken an illegal payment of nearly $1 million from a youth center's builder, then hid the money.

The panel of six men and six women also found Ciavarella guilty of "honest services mail fraud" and of being a tax cheat, for failing to list that money and more on his annual public financial-disclosure forms and on four years of tax returns. In addition, they found him guilty of conspiring to launder money. The jurors acquitted Ciavarella of extortion and bribery in connection with $1.9 million that prosecutors said the judges extracted from the builder and owner of two youth centers, including allegations that Ciavarella shared the proceeds of FedEx boxes that were stuffed with tens of thousands of dollars in cash.

Wilkes-Barre Area School District has its own sordid past with three top officials on the board being convicted to hard jail time. The Brockovich case and the "kids for cash" case have buoyed Holodick and the SOS group in believing that it ain't over until it is over.

Chapter 4 Bad Education & The WBA School Board

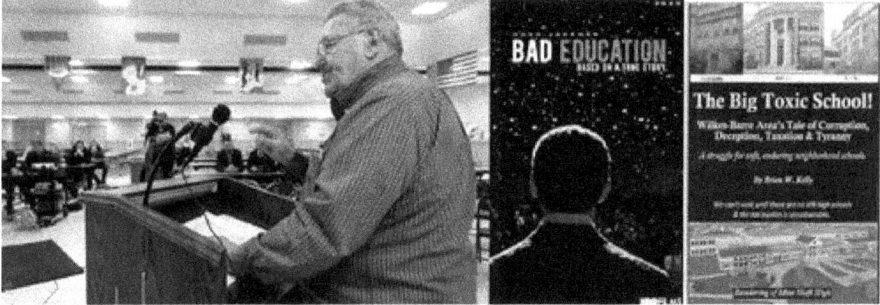

Dr. Richard Holodick, President of the Save Our Schools Group is passionate about the School district running on the up and up. Right now, to many of the residents of the Wilkes-Barre Area, this is not the case. It may not be as bad as the Scranton School District's corruption, but the minutes of board meetings have the same smell of corruption if you know what I mean. Things are so wrong; they just smell bad.

Just a month after the release of Kelly's book, The Big Toxic School in the fall 2019, and about eight years after the Conahan / Ciavarella Kids for Cash corruption debacle, a new movie called Bad Education made its world premiere on September 8, 2019 at the Toronto International Film Festival.

Brian Kelly, co-author and editor of the two-book set, has become convinced that if he and I can explain the corruption in the movie Bad Education, it will be easier for us to define corruption. Moreover, it will be easier to demonstrate corruption by citing the apparent crookedness that has been all too prevalent in the Wilkes-Barre School Board over the past twenty years--especially in the more recent Superintendent Brian Costello years. So, hang on, after we tell you about Bad Education, we will make the connection, and it will make a lot of sense.

Though there is not a lot of obvious sex and intrigue in the Wilkes-Barre Area School District's saga, there is a ton of wrongdoing in both Bad Education in the Roslyn School District and the Wilkes-Barre Area School District. If there is money hidden from the books and we think there is in WBASB, we have yet to find it but other than pure incompetence, nothing explains the mischief we uncover more than some stashed away look.

We immediately saw the connection between the two school districts. The Roslyn School District has gone down as the location in which the largest scandal ever in US School districts took place. The film Bad Education memorializes the events of the corrupt happenings It is based on a mid-2000s scandal in Roslyn, a well-off suburb of New York City.

The movie is real, not fictional. It tells the story of Superintendent Frank Tassone (recognized by fans as a brilliantly creepy Hugh Jackman). Tassone is a superficially charming and ambitious school superintendent who is arrested for embezzling millions from the school district. The case involved multiple arrests and millions of dollars, and would later become known as the largest school embezzlement scandal in U.S. history.

It cost Roslyn $11.2 million from the school budget. No comparison to WBASD. Hold on before that conclusion takes hold. The Washington street and Kistler projects alone cost the WBA taxpayers $6 million. It all went down the tubes. Nobody knows if that means that somebody has it stashed in their tube socks but don't dismiss that possibility. There were plenty more WBASD losses to follow.

Your authors see the potential malfeasance and misfeasance of the Wilkes-Barre Area School Board as deserving of similar punishment. Replacing the board next time around looks like a sure thing but the school building expenses will all be sunk costs by then and few businesses would want to buy a school built on a toxic mine shaft to run their organizations. Nonetheless, the film Bad Education offers hope that the WBASD real life scandal can be resolved in the taxpayers' favor and some prior beneficiaries may be located to fund making Wilkes-Barre School District whole again without its Big Toxic School. Now we're talking!

Holodick has expressed his desire to find a Hugh Jackman-like male lead and an Allison Janney female lead who would like to take a movie production cast on to similar success as Bad Education.

Tongue in cheek, Dr. Prevuznak (Prev) and Jackman do look somewhat alike. See below picture. For the record Dr. Prev was the most honest, hardworking God dedicated man I had ever worked with. He walked the walk.

Prev started in the classroom as an art teacher which paved the way for his coming up through the ranks as a principal, assistant superintendent and superintendent. The proceeds and the publicity for the WBASD taxpayers would go a long way in fighting the rigged WBASD system.

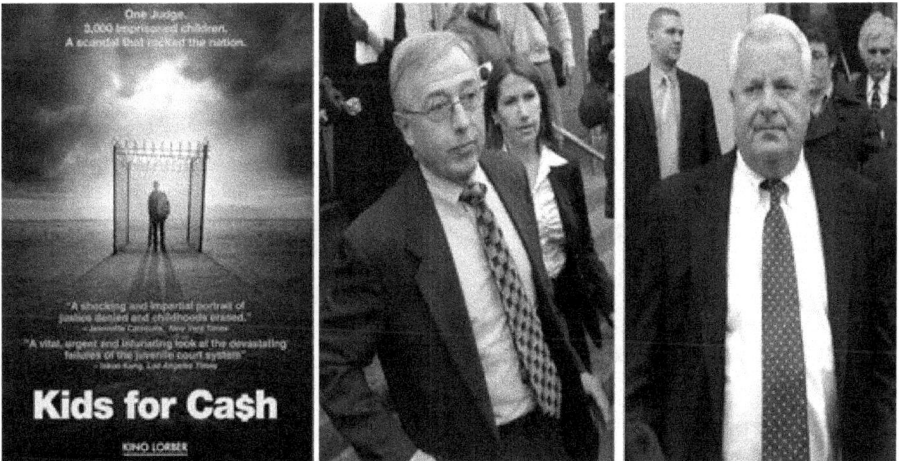

Over a September 2019 weekend, HBO released Bad Education. This Hugh Jackman-led film about a real-life school scandal that took place nearly two decades ago in an affluent suburb of Long Island lives on in the real people of Roslyn. The excellent screen play was written by Mike Makowsky.

Please indulge me as I tell that story and give me till later to make the full connection between the two sets of corruption. We hope we can give a great writer like Mike Makowsky some ideas that he can use to create a screen play from this two-book set, in much the same way as he was able finish his work for the movie Bad Education.

NEPA real criminal verdicts and sentences

On February 18, 2011, following a trial, a federal jury convicted NEPA Judge Mark Ciavarella on 12 of the 39 remaining counts that he faced including racketeering, a crime in which prosecutors said the former judge used children "as pawns to enrich himself." In convicting Ciavarella of racketeering, the jury agreed with prosecutors that he and cohort Judge Conahan had taken an illegal payment of nearly $1 million from a youth center's builder, then hid the money. Some say they hid the money in their wallets.

Using children as pawns is relevant to establishing a Taj Mahal for the purpose of a monument for the board or to achieve 6A sports designation—or perhaps to have a source of a lot of cash? Who really knows? ? Whatever the reason for this consolidation decision it was not education-based. So far it seems like a bad deal for everybody in the area except the board—or so it seems.

Our children got to play the role of pawns while our seniors got to fight the fights of their lives to save their homes as "pawns?" The panel of six men and six women also found Ciavarella guilty of "honest services mail fraud" and of being a tax cheat, for failing to list that money and more on his annual public financial-disclosure forms and on four years of tax returns.

Can we the people consider paying $55,000 an acre for land assessed at $10,000 an acre, "honest service fraud?" Or, overspending the operational budget by $10,000 in one year a violation of Code 609, never adjudicated as, honest services fraud?" "In addition, they found "Shiv" guilty of conspiring to launder money. The jurors acquitted Ciavarella of extortion and bribery in connection with $1.9

million that prosecutors said the judges extracted from the builder and owner of two youth centers, including allegations that Ciavarella shared the proceeds of FedEx boxes that were stuffed with tens of thousands of dollars in cash. They say officials have a hard time making a lot of money in jobs that have no salary unless they do a lot of building. Touche'

The Wilkes-Barre Area School District has its own sordid past with three top officials on the board being convicted to hard jail time. The Brockovich case and the "kids for cash" case have buoyed Holodick and the SOS group in believing that it ain't over until it is over.

Just a month after the release of Kelly's *The Big Toxic School* and about eight years after" Kids for Cash," the new movie called Bad Education made its world premiere on September 8, 2019 at the Toronto International Film Festival.

You can't help but see the connection between the kindred spirits in the districts. The question of the day is the WBASD today's Roslyn School District. Will enough cash be found in Wilkes-Barre or Plains to make the Roslyn $11.2 million heist look like small potatoes. We won't know unfortunately unless a state audit looks for something rather than looking the other way.

We like to remind our readers that malfeasance in office, or official misconduct, is the commission of an unlawful act, done in an official capacity, that affects the performance of official duties. Malfeasance in office is often the grounds for a just cause removal of an elected official by statute or a recall election (No recalls in PA law). The acts credited to the WBASB have the look and feel of Malfeasance in office. If not this then it has a scent of "misfeasance in office" which is the commission of a lawful act, performed in an official capacity, that improperly causes harm. Nonfeasance in is the failure to perform an official duty that is required such as getting the proper signoffs for a major dollar expenditure. Bet an audit would find a lot of all three.

The Save our Schools Group would like nothing more than to take the WBASD (Wilkes-Barre Area School District) to court to remove the board and stop the Big Toxic School in its tracks. However, in a word, they can't because of one big word – MONEY. SOS simply does not have the money. The group would need a lot more funds than what is available in its budget.

To repeat our greatest desires for the notoriety of the problems in WBA, it would be magical if we could find a Hugh Jackman-like male lead and an Allison Janney female lead who would like to take a movie production cast on to similar success as Bad Education. As noted, the proceeds and the publicity for the WBASD taxpayers would go a long way in fighting the rigged WBASD system.

Chapter 5 Historical Overview of Wilkes-Barre City

Wilkes-Barre is the 18th largest city in Pennsylvania and it serves as the county seat of Luzerne County. With a population of 321,423 Luzerne County is the 12th largest county in the Commonwealth of Pennsylvania in which there are 67 counties in total. There are two other names for the way the population including Wilkes-Barre is grouped. Both refer to the same city groups.

Wilkes-Barre is one of the principal cities in what is known as the Scranton–Wilkes-Barre–Hazleton, PA Metropolitan Statistical Area. Located at the center of the Wyoming Valley, which is also a pseudonym. Often abbreviated as WB, it is second in size to the nearby city of Scranton. The Scranton–Wilkes-Barre–Hazleton, PA Metropolitan Statistical Area had a population of 563,631 as of the 2010 Census, making it the fourth-largest metro/statistical area in the state of Pennsylvania. Therefore the population of the Wyoming Valley is also 563,631 since they refer to the same population.

The Wyoming Valley is a historic industrialized region of Northeastern Pennsylvania. As we will discuss in this book, it was once famous for fueling the industrial revolution in the United States with its many anthracite coal mines. As noted as a metropolitan area, it is known as the Scranton/Wilkes-Barre metropolitan area, after its principal cities, Scranton and Wilkes-Barre, and it is the 101st-largest metropolitan area in the United States and the 4th largest in Pennsylvania.

Wilkes-Barre and the surrounding Wyoming Valley are framed by the Pocono Mountains to the east, the Endless Mountains to the north and west, and the Lehigh Valley to the south. The "mighty" Susquehanna River flows through the entire state, through the center of the valley and it defines the northwestern border of the city. The River flows from upstate New York state to the Chesapeake Bay in Maryland. The North Branch begins as the outlet of Otsego Lake in Cooperstown, New York. At 444 mi long, it is the longest river on the American east coast and the 16th longest in the United States. Wilkes-Barre was founded in 1769 and formally incorporated in 1806.

The city grew rapidly in the 19th century after the discovery of nearby "black gold" coal reserves and the arrival of hundreds of thousands of immigrants who provided a labor force for the local mines.

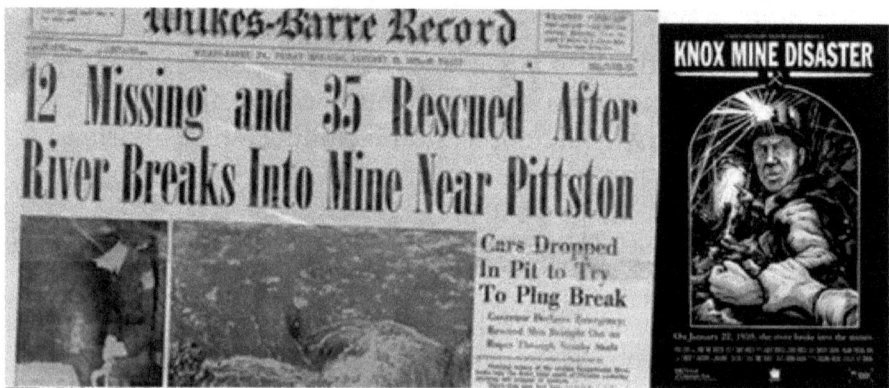

The City reached the height of its prosperity in the first half of the 20th century. Its population peaked at more than 86,000. Following World War II, the city's economy declined due to the collapse of industry. The Knox Mine disaster, a major event in the history of the area is discussed below. It accelerated this trend after large portions of the area's coal mines were flooded and could not be reopened.

Today, the city has a population of 40,569, making it the largest city in Luzerne County and the 18th-largest city in Pennsylvania.

Unfortunately, the financial and industrial prosperity and the population of the city have been continually declining. The elimination of all three high schools in the City is not expected to help matters at all.

The Wilkes-Barre School District was the forerunner of the Wilkes-Barre Area School District. There have been schools in Wilkes-Barre City for over 100 years. Wilkes-Barre City itself was founded in 1769 and formally incorporated in 1806. As noted, the city grew rapidly in the 19th century (1800's) after the discovery of nearby coal reserves and the arrival of hundreds of thousands of immigrants who provided a labor force for the local mines.

The coal mining fueled the industrialization in the city, which reached such as height of its prosperity in the early 20th century that Wilkes-Barre became known for a time as a boom town. Its population peaked at more than 86,000. However, following World War II, the city's economy declined due to the collapse of industry, including the mining industry.

As noted, one of the major disasters that precipitated the demise of the mines was known as the Knox Mine disaster. This disaster was a mining accident on January 22, 1959, at the River Slope Mine in Jenkins Township, Pennsylvania. It was due to mine bosses abusing the mining rules.

The disaster occurred when workers were ordered to dig illegally under the Susquehanna River without proper safety precautions. They mined too close to the surface thus creating a hole in the riverbed above the mines which caused the river to flood into the many interconnected mine galleries in the Wyoming Valley.

The mines were thus flooded between the right-bank (western shore) town of Exeter, Pennsylvania, and the left-bank (eastern shore) town of Port Griffith in Jenkins Township, near Pittston. Twelve miners were killed. Plugging the hole in the riverbed took three days, and mitigation efforts created several new islands between the two towns and altered the western-side flow of the Susquehanna River around these.

The coal industry in northeastern Pennsylvania had already been in decline at the time of the accident as oil and natural gas became more popular forms of energy. The Knox Mine disaster is considered to have been the proverbial nail in the coffin that virtually destroyed the coal mining industry in northeastern Pennsylvania. The mines could no longer be worked when such large portions of the area's coal mines were flooded from Susquehanna River water and could never be reopened.

It was a major loss for Wilkes-Barre and surrounding areas. For years Wilkes-Barre had prospered from the coal brought to the surface from these deep mines. Today, Wilkes-Barre has a population of just about 40,000, making it the largest city in Luzerne County and the 13th-largest city in Pennsylvania.

Wilkes-Barre for years has been the major city in the Wilkes-Barre School District. Two thirds of the School District residents live in Wilkes-Barre City proper. In all, the District serves Bear Creek Township, Borough of Bear Creek Village, Borough of Laflin, Buck Township, City of Wilkes-Barre, Laurel Run Borough, Plains Township and Wilkes-Barre Township. According to recent census data, the district serves a total resident population of over 60,000.

Considering that the Wilkes-Barre Area School District plans to move its high schools out of Wilkes-Barre City, you can imagine how residents of the largest residential area feel about having no high school presence in their city. At one time, there was a school board that cared what its constituent voters thought. Wilkes-Barre will be left with three beautiful unused high school buildings because the school board chose not to maintain them.

Wilkes-Barre students will begin to be bussed to Plains Township to attend high school when the Big Toxic School on the contaminated hill in Plains Twp. is completed. Let's begin talking about the high school situation by taking a trip down Memory Lane before there even was a high school in the area.

Remember when high school was new in Wilkes-Barre in 1867

On August 12, 2018, Tom Mooney tackled the history of schools in the Wilkes-Barre area in an opinion article he wrote for the Times Leader, a local newspaper. Tom began by discussing some of the new news on the school situation in 2018, noting that within a few years, the three Wilkes-Barre public high schools will be only memories.

He cited that in the prior week, the School Board (WBASB) had announced that the consolidation plan had been expanded to include all of them – Coughlin, GAR and Meyers – in the new combined high school planned for a site outside the Wilkes-Barre City limits in Plains Township. Wilkes-Barre Area residents know that the building of this complex, which many refer to as The Big Toxic School is already under construction.

Original Wilkes-Barre High School later Coughlin

When the consolidation project is completed, an era stretching back a century will have ended. There will be no high schools in Wilkes-Barre City. Mooney's article is a walk down memory lane that takes a short look at the long story of how the three high schools began. Wilkes-Barre itself was founded as previously noted in 1769. By the time the first high school was ready to be built as the City was beginning to grow, 98 years had passed from its founding. The population had grown to about 4,000. Students from the upper grades in Wilkes-Barre found something new when September of 1867 rolled around – their first-ever high school. They would no longer have to share a building with younger children.

The 1867 new high school building predated Wilkes-Barre High and Coughlin. It was small to say the least by today's standards. It was built on the first block of North Washington Street at Butler Alley. Mooney found some old maps showing that it occupied the space today utilized for a parking lot and the Coughlin High School gym. The teachers, according to records, were women from Philadelphia. Education in the Wyoming Valley was in its infancy.

Today there are more students in the Wilkes-Barre Area School District (WBASD) than the population of Wilkes-Barre when its first high school was built. Of course, there were not very many students in this first version of a Wilkes-Barre high school, but the city's population – driven by the anthracite industry – was just beginning to grow. From just a little over 4,000 in 1860, according to the U.S. Census, it would surpass 10,000 in 1870. The mines were the big catalyst for growth.

So fast was the growth, in fact, that the district's leaders decided to build a larger high school as soon as possible. In 1881, with the city's population having quickly soared past 23,000, the district opened a new school on East Union Street at North State Street. This building would remain as the Wilkes-Barre High School for three more decades and then, it too would need to be enlarged.

Once again, though, population growth drove local education. By 1900, Wilkes-Barre had 52,000 residents. Plans were laid to build a third and still larger high school. Business was booming with unprecedented growth. The site chosen for the third new high school was the first block of North Washington Street, between Butler Alley and East Union. Construction soon began, and by 1909 the massive building that still stands there was opened. It was the largest school building in the area. When the District decommissioned this building several years ago, the historical society had the building registered as the oldest high school in the state of Pennsylvania.

There were other parts of the city – namely the Heights and West End (today's South Wilkes-Barre) – which were beginning to grow rapidly. The growth was not about to end any time soon and so the officials decided to build a new high school in each of those sections, one right after the other.

Amazing! what most Wilkes-Barre residents think of as the old Coughlin High School was established in 1890 after this small school had been operational as Wilkes-Barre High School. The current school structure had been scheduled to be built on the original school's site in 1905, but due to a flood—which affected the entire basement and first floor, the building had to be restarted. Eventually it was completed, and the building was opened unofficially on September 11, 1911. It was formally dedicated in October 1912.

A second part of the building, called the Annex, was built in 1955 and formally dedicated on November 2, 1955. The main building which was once Wilkes-Barre High School has four floors, a basement, and an attic, and the Annex has three stories with a partial basement. Id did not matter to the caretaker board that it was the oldest active public school in Pennsylvania, having been built in 1909.

Yes, dear readers, the older of the two buildings that makes up Coughlin is over 110 years old. The second building is about 60 years old. With the construction of a second-high school in Wilkes-Barre in 1925, the building name was changed from Wilkes-Barre High and dedicated as James M. Coughlin High School in memory of Superintendent James Martin Coughlin, who served in that capacity from 1890 to 1918.

The main building was closed on December 23, 2015, after 104 years of continuous use. This came as a result of a lengthy series of meetings by the Wilkes-Barre Area School Board, where it was decided that Coughlin and another Wilkes-Barre Area High School (Elmer L. Meyers Junior/Senior High School) would close and combine after the Coughlin site was to be closed and rebuilt. The Annex building would continue to house 11th and 12th graders until the new school is built and 9th and 10th grades students placed in a recently renovated former Mackin Elementary School building, and the 11th and 12th graders will be placed in the old Times Leader building next to Coughlin.

Of course, the WBASB has a history of making decisions when it has no authority. It did not have zoning approval for the new site in

Wilkes-Barre and so after blowing $6 million on preparatory activities, zoning was denied.

Construction of the proposed but unapproved by zoning Washington Street Consolidated School Complex was expected to be completed by early 2018, when both former high schools would converge in the new school. However, the Board was unable to move forward with the plan to use the Coughlin site. Then what? After this miss-step, the board was aggravated at Wilkes-Barre City for not granting zoning wavers that the Board should not have expected. The Superintendent Brian Costello vowed not to build in Wilkes-Barre in a spite move. Refurbishing the three forever schools was deemed by Costello then to be out of the question.

WBA has 117 sq. miles and district owned property to select a site. They select a coal-mine, coal ash toxic dump. Little concern for the safety of the children and staff. They pay 5 x the lowest assessed value, & $3.2 M for un-assessed mineral rights that could be worth zero. They purchased un-reclaimed land and are building on un-reclaimed land. No concern for the taxpayers and so irresponsible there needs to be an investigation.

So, in another rebound play, on March 5, 2018, the Board voted to purchase land in Plains, Pennsylvania for a new merged massive consolidated high school. The plans have faced vocal opposition because of all the wasted money and many other reasons including its being built on a toxic mine dump. This Big Toxic School has still not been accepted by residents who want to go back to the three city High School days.

Chapter 6 Historical Overview of the 3 City High Schools

Some more good stuff about Coughlin

There are bits and pieces of Wilkes-Barre education history that can be found in various places. For example, the history of Coughlin High School, the successor school to Wilkes-Barre High School is documented in the school's 1990 school yearbook. "That was our anniversary year and for that reason, I thought we should have the history in our yearbook," retired social studies teacher Donald Devans said.

Devans, 80, of Dallas, graduated from Coughlin in 1954. He worked at Coughlin from 1960 to 1997 and the book was a personal task to write about the school's history in the 1990 yearbook. "I decided I should put it together, and I took different sources of stuff that was written in the school and tried to combine it together," Devans said. "We took pictures that we found and had them reproduced and put into the story."

It was the school's 100th anniversary that year. When the school was incorporated in 1890, it was known as Wilkes-Barre High School and occupied a building on the corner of Washington and Union streets. Only the third floor was used for high school. The remainder of the building was used as the Union Street Grammar School.
In 1896, the Union Grade School was built on the same property and the first structure would later be known as the "Old Building." Construction on a new high school across North Washington Street began in 1909.

It opened in 1911. The cost of the four-floor building was $470,816.97.

The school was renamed James M. Coughlin High School in 1925 after Wilkes-Barre opened a second high school -- GAR. James M. Coughlin served as superintendent of city schools from 1890 to 1918. Coughlin High School kept red and blue as school colors and the school symbol of "Crusader."

The rear of the new high school building contained the auditorium. The exterior walls were constructed of Indiana limestone on a base of red stone from Laurel Run quarries near Wilkes-Barre.

"Coughlin is an imposing symmetrical neo-classicist limestone building with projecting end bays and an ornamented language of cornice projections, balustraded parapets and keystones flat arches sitting atop a rusticated ground floor level," a 2014 feasibility report on school district building options says. "The building is a substantial piece of construction by any measure, replete with architectural value."

In the parlance of those who debate renovating schools or replacing them, the old Coughlin School building is a major vote for renovating this "forever school," so that it will last forever. And it will if some fool with no concern for history does not rip it down first. We prove it time and time again in this two-volume book set, there is no need to build a new school when the WBASD has Coughlin, Gar, and Meyers in its real estate inventory.

The Coughlin school basement included a gymnasium and 10 rooms. On the first floor were offices for the superintendent of schools, the school board, their secretary, the supervisor of drawing, and the high school matron. The principal's office was on the second floor.

At the rear of the Union Street building, a power plant was installed to provide light, heat and ventilation in the new high school, the old high school and the Union Street Grammar building. An underground subway with steam pipes and electric wires connected the power plant to the high school buildings.

"People don't realize this building was heated by steam heat," current Coughlin Principal Pat Patte said. "If you notice in front of the street, Washington Street, it doesn't get snow. It melts because the old steam

heat runs underneath it. There isn't much snow because the street is so warm."
Devans, a Coughlin student from 1948 to 1954 noted that Coughlin still used the old buildings across the street in the 1950s.

For example, there was a third building across the street that was put to good use until 1972, the year of the Agnes Flood in Wilkes-Barre and surrounds. Its use was for administrative offices and classrooms, The administration building was on land that currently is used as Coughlin's parking lot. When the yearbook article author Devans commented on the older buildings he said "I used the buildings across the street. They have long since gone."

In 1955, Coughlin added the annex to the main school along North Washington Street. The annex, shown below, included a new gymnasium, dental unit, washroom, cafeteria, homemaking unit, band room, locker rooms, shower rooms and 12 new classrooms.

The Annex

Coughlin High School Expansion—the Annex

The school board voted to borrow $1.7 million to fund renovations at Coughlin and build the annex. Jacob P. Breidinger served as school principal from 1901 to 1931 and was the school's longest-serving principal. The school yearbook was first published in 1924 and became "the Breidlin" in 1925. The name was formed from the first syllable of Breidinger's last name and the last syllable of Coughlin's last name.

A regional school called GAR Memorial High School opened in 1925 in the Heights neighborhood in the city and also served students from the Mayflower and Rolling Mill Hill neighborhoods in the city. In 1930, the city began building a third high school, Elmer L. Myers High School, in South Wilkes-Barre.

Meyers and GAR began as neighborhood-based schools that allowed students to walk to school, and for the short-haul at least, they still operate as neighborhood schools today though their future is very much in doubt. The completion of the ongoing construction of the Big Toxic School is destined to end their use.

Coughlin has always been a more regional school, but it too is short lived. In 1911, Coughlin was centrally located for its student population coming from both the north and south ends of the city. Before the formation of the Wilkes-Barre Area School District in 1972, students from Laurel Run, Bear Creek Township and Bucks Township went to Coughlin on a tuition basis from their respective school districts.

There was a time when neighboring communities believed that Mayor Tom McGroarty of Wilkes-Barre was checking out the boundaries of WB City. Nearby burgs were concerned that McGroarty wanted to be Mayor of a larger area. In 1927, Parsons and Miners Mills boroughs were annexed into the city and the former borough high schools became grade schools. The high school students from these former independent communities enrolled at Coughlin.

Students attending Coughlin in 1972 came from seven different municipalities — Bear Creek Township, Buck Township, Laflin, Laurel Run, Plains Township, Wilkes-Barre Township, and parts of Wilkes-Barre. In 1972, the high schools of Wilkes-Barre Township and Plains Township became junior high schools.

"The present Coughlin High School has some unusual characteristics," as Devans wrote in the 1990 yearbook. "It is an urban school but not a neighborhood school. Out of the 1,097 students that attended Coughlin proper for example, 807 rode buses to school." Flood damage GAR and Meyers students are mostly walkers—for now!

Coughlin sustained major damage from the two floods of the Susquehanna River. The St. Patrick's Day Flood of 1936 caused Coughlin to be closed from March 18 to March 25. Kelly's wife noted that it might have been possible that the flood occurred from human liquid waste discharged on the biggest Irish celebration of the year. Those of other descents and nationalities saw this as possibilit but believed the rain was a more causal agent.

Floodwaters wreak havoc on wood. They warped the gym floor and the paper books never look the same when air dried. The water destroyed stored books and knocked out cafeteria motors. The Hurricane Agnes flood in June 1972 caused even more extensive damage to the basement and first floor of both buildings.

The loss of supplies and equipment was estimated at $700,000. Because of the severity of the damage, officials delayed the opening of the school year to mid-September.

In May 2014, the school district installed protective scaffolding along the exterior of Coughlin by its main and secondary entrances due to exterior deterioration. Of course another course of action could have been to fix the problem or to have had a maintenance program that caught the problem before it became an issue, but this board has a one word maintenance strategy of which all residents of WBA are now aware—Neglect.

FYI, later that month, officials discovered exterior deterioration at Meyers High School and decided to spend more than $400,000 on a feasibility study of district building options. Your authors believe this explanation of a discovery because without normal maintenance inspections problems pop up and are never solved before they occur.

The school board looked around for a solution to the Meyers problem and wound up having to solve a deeper Coughlin program. The real problem of course was the board's lack of maintenance on all district buildings in their care. When no maintenance is the strategy something breaking becomes the emergency of the day. Nobody in WBA would run their homes this way.

But, when your budget is over $100 million dollars, you may think your options are unlimited—especially if you know nothing about taking care of property so it will last. Without blinking an eye, the "neglect" board approved plans to spend $8 million to renovate a school in mothballs. How fortuitous that the board could ask the moths to leave so it could remodel the shuttered Mackin elementary school to become the backup location for Coughlin students in the event Coughlin were to close. How convenient for bad management to be rewarded for its neglect.

In June 2015, in what some call "the board meeting from hell," the school board approved a plan to merge Coughlin and Meyers high schools into a new building on the current Coughlin site. Everybody knew there would be a lot of building construction going on if this folly of a plan passed muster and if it survived the gauntlet it faced. It did not survive as well it should not have.

In January, the Wilkes-Barre Area School Board (WBASB) chose to close Coughlin's main building (the one with all the history) and moved roughly 500 students in 11th and 12th grades into the building known as The Annex.

See Mackin School. The ninth and 10th grades moved into what had by then become known as the renovated Mackin school in the city's

East End. The Mackin "insurance policy work" had been completed and the board decided it would become the beneficiary.

The district hired crews to clean out the main building and prepare for the historic building's demolition. Nobody reported on demolition kickbacks being offered but the public and the Historical Society wondered why the board would rip down the oldest operational high school building in Pennsylvania if there were not a prize attached to such a misdeed?

I am very saddened," Devans said. "The memories of the students and the past and individuals who graduated, it's sad to see the old things go. The younger generation they don't see it that way, maybe. I don't think you build schools like the old ones. There is so much in that building." Facts for this piece were provided by mbuffer@citizensvoice.com; The authors extend our sincer thank you.

Tell me just a little more about Coughlin High School's History.

When this was written, in this year, the Coughlin High School History Club is in its sixth year as a club. It was started by seniors from the class of 2015 who were interested in history. The club sold t-shirts as its first fundraiser. As the club evolves, it is hoping to participate in community service events and even plan field trips to different historic destinations.

Trivia About Coughlin

Below are some interesting bits of trivia which the CHS History Club compiled. They provide them to all for your personal enjoyment.

1. 1890, oldest high school in Wilkes-Barre, Union Street High School $56,000
2. 1896, Union Street Grade School built on same location, high school entered on N Washington St, Grade school entered through E. Union St.
3. Two schools were connected with a bridge
4. Wilkes-Barre High School began construction in 1909 (where CHS is now), first occupied in 1911, $470,816.97

5. First clubs were literary societies, Cliosophic and Sorosis formed in 1895
6. 1925, building dedicated in the name of the first Superintendent James M. Coughlin
7. 1955, construction was completed on the "Annex", $1,743,000
8. School was flooded in 1972
9. The Journal is the longest continuously published high school newspaper in the U.S., it began approximately in 1892
10. Today Coughlin made up of 7 municipalities
11. First graduating class had 10 students
12. 15 total principals in history, first was TJ McConnon,
13. JP Briedinger was longest running principal
14. School yearbook was first published in 1924 named Briedlin, combination of Briedlinger and Coughlin
15. The Coughlin Alma Mater was written by Bessie Stella Jones class of 1907
16. After Coughlin High School became operational, came GAR – named Grand Army of the Republic Memorial High School

By 1925 the Heights had a school, named GAR Memorial (a bow to the Civil War veterans' group Grand Army of the Republic). Almost immediately, work began on the third school and by 1930 it was open, honoring school board member Dr. Elmer L. Meyers. The old Wilkes-Barre High School was renamed for former superintendent James M. Coughlin. GAR, a local high school was only one in the nation named after Grand Army of the Republic.

May 18, 2015 Times Leader

Where did GAR come from? Wilkes-Barre was booming in its infancy. In 1921, plans for a new junior-senior high school were moving along. The big question was, what to name it? Three members of the school board were sons of Civil War soldiers. One of them –John A. Hourigan — proposed "Grand Army of the Republic." It was a nickname for U.S. military forces during the 1861-1865 conflict and the name taken by a veterans group.

It is a unique name. So unique, that a comprehensive online list of American public high schools shows no other school shares the name. GAR Memorial High School "Every member of the board approved, and the structure came to be known as the GAR Memorial High School."as the district announced in the building's dedicatory booklet of 1925.

Ninety years later, in the sesquicentennial year of the end of the Civil War, the school still stands, and its name still conjures memories of the blue-uniformed troops who saved the American union.

Some more facts about Wilkes-Barre and its high schools:

GROWTH IN NUMBERS

Early in the 20th century, the city of Wilkes-Barre was prosperous and growing steadily. Figures in the "Wilkes-Barre Record Almanac" show between 1900 and 1910, the population increased from 51,000 to 67,000. The surge was driven by the anthracite coal industry, and by 1920 reached 73,000. Annexing nearby towns pushed the figure to about 87,000 by the end of the 1920s. The public-school system was overburdened. Along with population growth, more students stayed in school the full 12 years. By the end of the second decade of the century, more than 12,000 students were enrolled in the system, nearly 2,000 of them crowded into the Wilkes-Barre High School (now known as Coughlin).

So, the forward-thinking school district of the post-World War I era found a solution: build two new junior high schools for the fastest growing parts of the city. The first was in the Heights, the second was in South Wilkes-Barre.

HONORING THE SOLDIERS

The Region's Civil War veterans, their ranks diminishing rapidly, had long advocated some sort of recognition for their beloved Grand Army of the Republic. The largest GAR group in the area was the Conyngham Post 97. Housed in a magnificent, castle-like building on South Main Street, its priority was campaigning for a memorial clock tower on Public Square. Grand Army of the Republic (GAR)

Building on South Main Street Wilkes-Barre PA.

Some disliked that idea, preferring to keep the square open. Others pushed the idea of honoring the old vets by dedicating the newly planned Market Street Bridge.

It was against that background that Hourigan, also a journalist who owned the daily Wilkes-Barre Evening News, proposed the Civil War-related name for the new Heights school.

By autumn 1922, the structural framework of the building was in place. On October 14, four uniformed Civil War veterans laid the cornerstone. GAR Commander A.H. Brown drew the eras together when he proclaimed the school "a monument to the heroism of the past and a storehouse of knowledge for the future. The school's location carried the Civil War theme further.

Old maps show, by the late 19th century, the city gave names of prominent Civil War personalities to cross streets in the Heights section. The new school was between streets honoring generals Grant and Sherman, part of a grid bearing names of Lincoln, Welles (secretary of the Navy) and generals Hancock, Meade, Sheridan and Custer. Bet you did not know that?

THE NAMING AND DEDICATION

In the autumn of 1925, GAR Memorial High School was operational. On Nov. 21, it was dedicated in an elaborate ceremony presided over by Dr. Elmer L. Meyers, the school board president who led the project to completion. Hourigan became the vice president.

The original student body of 1,500 had found a palatial structure, with marble flooring and sweeping staircases, the railings and light fixtures made of bronze. A towering plaque, designed by 14-year-old Sarah Hughes, portrayed a robed figure, representing education, giving a laurel wreath to a Civil War soldier and simultaneously handing a torch of learning to a young woman.

Ringing the auditorium were windows designed as memorials to the titans of western culture. The choice of distinctive Civil War Union blue and Confederate gray as the school's colors was inevitable. The front featured a huge stone porch topped by a high arch, suggesting the building was fit to serve as a towering national monument.

The dedicatory booklet reminded visitors it was "a great school structure, named for the boys who stood firm in the days that tried men's souls." With the construction of Meyers High School in South Wilkes-Barre a few years later, the city's school district took on the form familiar to succeeding generations. Hourigan saw his Evening News newspaper merge with The Times Leader in 1939 and eventually he became chairman of board of the Wilkes-Barre Publishing Co. He died in 1951.

Elmer L. Meyers was honored by the naming of Wilkes-Barre's third high school for him in 1930. A staff physician at Wilkes-Barre General Hospital, he died in 1936.

The last of the four Civil War veterans who laid the cornerstone, Charles Rhenard, died in 1939. The South Main Street GAR Hall became a theater and office building. It was torn down in the '60s as part of an urban redevelopment program. The space is now a parkade.

Troubled by its now-aging junior and senior high schools, the Wilkes-Barre Area School District has studied various modernization possibilities, including building a new centralized senior high school.

The future of Wilkes-Barre Area's three big and historic buildings – Coughlin, GAR and Meyers — is still uncertain in everybody's mind but the determined school board who want nothing short of the destruction of all three grand high school buildings in Wilkes-Barre with a huge complex out of the city in Plains Township that is irreverently referred to as The Big Toxic High School.

For years, the district supported three high schools whose names are very familiar today but with the Big Toxic School construction well underway, it is clear that unless the Save Our Schools group with Dr. Richard Holodick serving as President succeeds, Wilkes-Barre PA will be without a high school within the City's borders and the bus lines will be getting a major shot in the arm to tote students up the big hill from Wilkes-Barre to Plains Twp.

The school building boom was fortunate, because in the 1920s the city of Wilkes-Barre expanded itself by absorbing the adjacent boroughs of Parsons and Miners Mills. This brought the City's population to more than 86,000 by 1930.

Even though some young people were still leaving school early to work, the total number of students grew by leaps and bounds up through the 1930s. Brian Kelly, coauthor, notes that his father, born in 1915, graduated from Coughlin High School shortly after it superseded Wilkes-Barre High School.

Meyers High praised in a student essay

History of Elmer L. Meyers High School remembered
By Lydia McFarlane,
Newspaper in Education student columnist, Jun 4, 2019
Updated Jun 18, 2020

As the doors begin to close on the reign of grand old Elmer L. Meyers High School, it is time we take a look back and remember the history of the place that has impacted so many for decades. It is hard to believe that a school opened in 1930 is still standing and very much still "Steadfast Forever" so many decades later.

It's no secret that the spirit of Meyers is something that is carried with you all throughout life. Many alumni feel the touch of Meyers in their hearts far into their adult lives. Blue and gold will forever live on in the veins of everyone who has come into contact with the school, but the spirit is not all that needs preserving.

The history of Meyers is something not often talked about, and as new doors start to open for the Wilkes-Barre Area School District, it is our duty as a community to never let the history of Meyers die along with the school. The school was opened in 1930, a true Depression-era school. It took four years of planning and work to build the now local monument.

LYDIAMCFARLANE Meyers News

The building spreads over three acres. The prominent main stairway is made of marble, specifically, "Giallo D'Istria, from Italy." Meyers was seen as a feat of modern architecture and technology, and it was something the people of the City were very proud to see built. According to the school's dedication program, the school was said to be, "a Depression-era construction project.

The school embodies the grand design of early 20th-century public architecture." It was "dedicated to community progress," says an original dedication to Meyers High, which it indeed succeeded in doing. It helped the city to move forward and really become much more of a community. According to this same dedication, "It is the gift of the people ... to the youth of Wilkes-Barre that opportunity may increase, education advance, and patriotic citizenship be founded."

An original post card of Elmer L. Meyers, 1937.

On Monday, Sept. 15, 1930, the new school was opened to all. The leaders of the school board and the entire community wanted to take steps forward for equality and modernism, as they did not discriminate against anyone in times of prejudice and hatred. "... it is dedicated as an institution of learning, knowing no sect, no creed, no color, erected by the children of yesterday for their children of today ..."

Dr. Elmer L. Meyers was described as, "The original prospector, who staked out the first claim and left the following proof." He was chosen to be honored following the trend established within the Wilkes-Barre Area School District where they gave names to school buildings in recognition of community service.

Dr. Meyers was a teacher, a distinguished physician, a 20-year member of the school board, and head of the Teachers' Committee for 15 years. His "record and his exemplary citizenship make Dr. Meyers outstanding in service and worthy of the honor conferred upon him."

Now, decades later, Elmer L. Meyers is a household name for people in our community. The respect and honor that people feel for a man from so long ago is immense. His legacy will forever live on in the hearts of all Mohawks and as the name of the school we all have come to know and love.

As we make our way to change and newness, we are at risk of forgetting what it is that got us to where we are today. It is important to always remember the history of a building that has given so much to our community over decades. It would not be fair to the amazing place that Meyers is today to just forget about its great history and how it came to be.

The name Elmer L. Meyers is one we should say with reverence, as without him, our great school would not be the same. It is time for the rich history of our beautiful school to run side by side with the blue and gold that will forever course through our veins.

More on Meyers

By the early 21st century, the school was seen to be in disrepair from apparent neglect, with safety structures in the form of scaffolding and wooden barriers erected in front of building facades. Moreover, major repairs were needed for the attached Memorial Stadium.

The Board, whose leadership was not from Wilkes-Barre per se, hated Wilkes-Barre City and was out to get Meyers right from the start. They promoted false stories that Meyers was not physically sound.

Yet, when the Board's construction projects were not permitted by Wilkes-Barre City Zoning, somehow, the Board then said that Meyers was sound enough to stay on as a major high school until their new Big Toxic School built on contaminated land was a "go!"

The people did not understand the on again off-again nature of a major city high school

Meyers got its new breath of life when on June 10, 2016, the Wilkes-Barre Area School Board voted to consolidate the local schools, merging Meyers and Coughlin into a new 9th through 12th grade school to be built on the Coughlin site in downtown Wilkes-Barre. The 7th and 8th grades were to be merged with Kistler Elementary to make that into a K-8th school (ie a middle school). The Board was ready to do anything to have its way.

However, it was unable to move forward with the plan to use the Coughlin site or another site in Wilkes-Barre which included the old Times Leader Building. The superintendent was really upset at Wilkes-Barre about it refusing its zoning request. So, in February 2018, the Board hemmed and hawed about the possibility of using Meyers as a middle school.

Then, on March 5, 2018, the Board voted to purchase land in Plains Township, Pennsylvania for the merged consolidated Taj Mahal Big Toxic High School. There is a lot of information in this book about the Plains transaction and most of it does not pass the smell test. The sniffers who checked out the board's actions found a lot wrong with their thinking. Could there have been some favoritism and unlawful actions so the board could have its way without following its own by-laws?

The plans have faced vocal opposition from many of the people for by adding GAR High School to the mix it would leave Wilkes-Barre City, the largest municipality in Luzerne County with no high schools at all. How could that help the city with the largest tax base in the county? The people did not like it one bit.

There were counter proposals with some suggesting that the school be turned into a charter school.[The school has been listed as an "At Risk" for historic preservation location by Preservation Pennsylvania, who noted that "[a]s a Depression-era construction project, the school embodies the grand design of early 20th-century public architecture. It serves a diverse neighborhood and is in a central location that children can walk to." Normal human beings cannot figure out why the board took the actions it did directly against the people's wishes.

Coughlin, GAR, and Meyers are all beautiful schools that the WBASB neglected until they became maintenance issues. They are still sturdy enough to be refurbished and used forever when the Big Toxic School fails to receive its occupancy permit.

Until the Board cuts over to the construction project of the Big Toxic School, and possibly gains its undeserved occupancy, Meyers & GAR and the Coughlin replacement will continue to provide education to approximately 898 students in grades 7–12. Its teacher ratio is good at approximately 12.6 students per teacher. Besides the marble staircases and the granite hallways, the auditorium is adorned with copious stained glass. None of this richness of the 1930's is included in the construction of the Big Toxic Consolidated School, which looks like it is designed by Lionel's Plasticville Engineers.

For a zillion years, the student body of Meyers has collectively been referred to as the "Mohawks". Meyers has many traditions that are still practiced today including a Moving Up Day, a ceremony that officially marks the junior class move to senior status, as well as the senior class moving to the stage for graduation, which happens the day after in the school's auditorium. The school also celebrates senior tea, a tradition that was started in the 1930s.

Coughlin, GAR and Meyers are neighborhood schools which is the preferred type of school in modern times. They require minimal to no bussing and the facilities are close enough that students can engage in activities without requiring bus rides to / from home events.

Smaller neighborhood schools such as Meyers, according to experts and reinforced by Dr. Richard Holodick, a national expert with impeccable credentials, tend to do a better job of making students feel connected. Studies have documented better relationships are likely to occur in smaller settings. "Students feel supported and cared for," they assert.

Copious research has shown reduced rates of student participation in extra-curricular activities in larger schools, Holodick noted. And there are concerns about kids getting lost in the largeness. That my friends is a big reason why the Save our Schools group has been lobbying for years for the neighborhood v consolidated approach. But it is not the only reason.

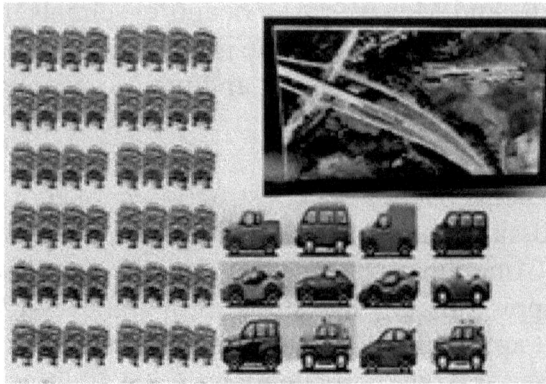

There are many. One example is bussing as the district goes from bussing 35% of the students to 95%. Due to the 117 square miles, some students can spend as much as two hours a day on a school bus; ground zero for bullying; two hours of non-instructional hours.

This site for all practical purposes is isolated--sandwiched between River/Maffet streets and North Main Street. Getting over 60 busses and student and faculty staff's cars, and delivery trucks in and out at peak hours may be difficult if not impossible. A traffic flow study could have negated the contaminated isolated site. It is highly questionable why the Plains township zoning board didn't require a traffic flow report prior to approving the project. There is a large hospital one mile away on River Street that has emergency vehicles that need free passage at 7:30 am at River street, Cross Valley exit.

Children / Students thrive in an environment where faculty, staff and fellow students know their names and who they are. This opportunity does not exist in a centralized school. In a neighborhood school, students have less chance of falling through the cracks because of this familiarity, and there is less risk of being overlooked. Smaller schools feel like a second "family" to students – not an industrial warehouse or in this case, a Big Toxic School of which to be concerned for one's health.

Chapter 7. Meyers Historical Resource Survey

For PA Bureau for Historic Preservation.
Prepared by: Lawrence M. Newman, AICP Executive Director
Diamond City Partnership 4 Public Square Wilkes-Barre, PA 18702
Editor: This chapter formalizes the notion of E.L. Meyers High school and its fine design and tasteful workmanship. This building is what is called today a "forever school" in contrast to the Lionel Train-type Plastic Ville model schools that are built as replacements.

Instead of schools that are designed to last forever, today's schools such as the big consolidated toxic school being built outside of Wilkes-Barre to replace Meyers, Coughlin, & GAR, is to last about forty years when it will have to be replaced.

The Original Plasticville School House

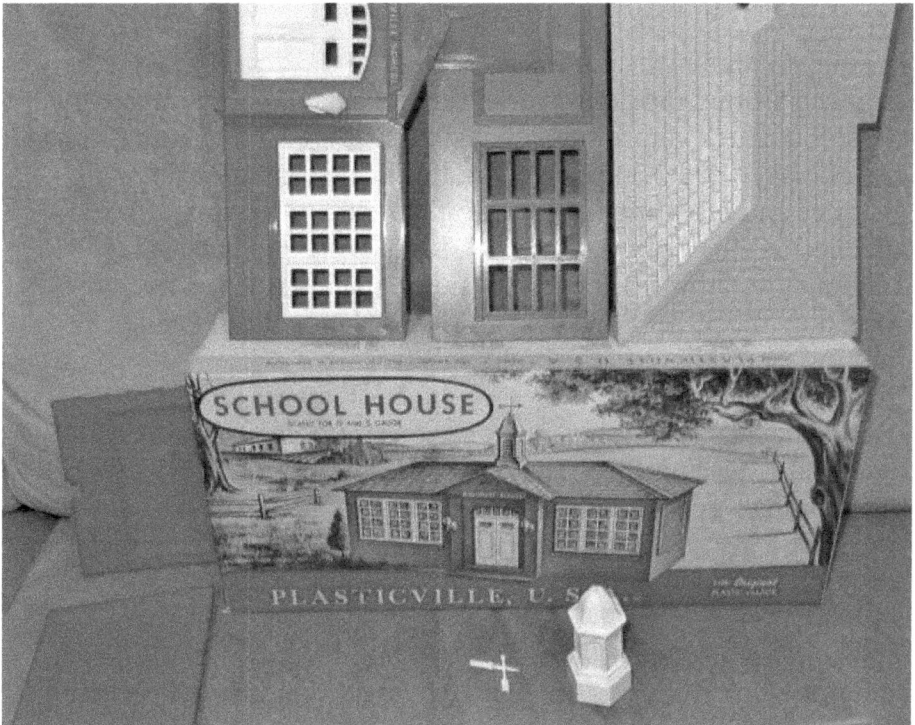

The Original Plasticville School House is more than likely made of similar material as the Big Toxic School except the Red School House will probably last longer than the new consolidated school. Just saying! Meyers High School, constructed as a junior-senior high school for the Wilkes-Barre City School District in the late 1930's, continues to serve its original function.

Built in the Firwood section of South Wilkes-Barre, on the site of the old Catlin Farm, it was designed to accommodate 2,200 students. The building's distorted pentagonal plan is cleverly shaped to take advantage of an irregular urban site that is dominated by the important intersection of Carey Avenue and Hanover Street, two major South Wilkes-Barre thoroughfares.

The school's rounded entrance portico at that intersection is designed to command the view along Hanover Street as one proceeds west past Geisinger South Wilkes-Barre (originally Mercy) Hospital, and along Carey Avenue as one proceeds northeast from Firwood Park. The building occupies 3 acres, with the remaining 4 acres containing the adjoining Wilkes-Barre Memorial Stadium.

In plan, the building's parti is comprised of three major elements arranged around the perimeter of the site: a three-story double-loaded classroom block whose splayed wings, set parallel to Carey Avenue and Hanover Street, are hinged around the building's primary entrance and monumental central stairwell; a three-story block, attached to the Carey Avenue classroom wing and containing the building's auditorium and gymnasium; and a single-loaded rear classroom block, set at 90 degrees to the Hanover Street wing and fronting the stadium to the building's west.

A subsidiary interior wing, containing classrooms and the building's natatorium, tees off the west side of the auditorium block, dividing the building's pentagonal interior court into three smaller light wells. The building's power plant occupies a separate building to the east of the auditorium wing.

The building's primary façade, clad in buff brick above an Indiana limestone water table, is dominated by two monumental porticoes: one, marking the building's main entrance, at the intersection of Carey and Hanover; and the other, at the eastern end of the building's Carey Avenue elevation, denoting the entrance to the high school's auditorium and gymnasium.

Both monumental porticoes feature three-story stone Corinthian columns set below a giant entablature, which also caps the classroom wings. The remainder of the building's street facade is fenestrated with rows of ganged windows separated into bays by plain brick pilasters. The building's original brick parapet, together with an elaborate balustrade above the two porticoes, was removed in recent years because of concerns about structural deterioration.

The building's west façade, while not as heroic in design as the Carey Avenue and Hanover Street facades, creates an imposing backdrop to Wilkes-Barre Memorial Stadium. The stadium itself sits well below street level, permitting direct access from the locker rooms in the basement of the western wing to the adjacent playing field. A concrete deck, extending the length of the western elevation, once provided direct access to the stadium home-side bleachers (also recently demolished).

Physical Description and Integrity (Item 38)
The school building incorporates several significant interior spaces. The first of these is the primary stair hall, a grandly scaled space immediately adjoining the school's main entrance and featuring a monumental double-return main staircase rising the full height of the building. The stair hall walls and the stair's treads and balustrades are clad in Giallo D'Istrio marble; decorative art glass windows provide illumination.

Stained Glass Ceiling in the Auditorium (art glass laylight)

The auditorium is another significant interior space. Accommodating 1,650, it features a proscenium stage and a rectangular main floor beneath a raked C-shaped balcony. The auditorium ceiling is dominated by an enormous art glass laylight with a border comprised of the state seals of each of the 48 states of the union at the time of the school's construction.

The auditorium's arcaded sidewalls, clad in walnut, feature eight additional art glass panels depicting a series of significant events in American history: "The Landing of Columbus;" "Signing of the Treaty with the Indians and William Penn," Washington at Valley Forge," Signing of the Declaration of Independence;" "Lincoln's Gettysburg Address," "Roosevelt at San Juan Hill," "Landing of the Pilgrims," and "The Return of the Soldiers with General Pershing from the World War," All of the building's art glass is the work of the Payne Studios of Paterson, New Jersey.

The building's other primary interior spaces include a gymnasium, a natatorium, a cafeteria, and industrial arts rooms. These, together with all of the building's classrooms, are linked by a series of stacked corridors featuring iron-spot brick wainscot and built-in display cases. In the academic blocks, the corridors are double-loaded with classrooms on either side; those facing the building's interior courts are generously fenestrated. While many of these rooms and spaces have undergone cosmetic modifications, they continue to reflect the design ethos of the Progressive Era.

Despite interior modifications such as the painting of portions of the brick wainscot lining the building's corridors, the 1970's replacement of original wood and steel sash windows along the school's street elevations, and the more recent removal of Meyers' original ornamental balustrades and parapet, the building still maintains its design integrity, along with almost all of its major character-defining features.

History and Significance (Item 38)

The Elmer L. Meyers Junior/Senior High School ("Meyers High School") is an intact example of a monumental Beaux-Arts urban high school of the early 20th-century, designed to extend the availability of secondary public education to coal-age Wilkes-Barre's expanding southern neighborhoods. Built from 1926 to 1930, it was the final major achievement of Wilkes-Barre's most important school architect, Robert Ireland. It was built at a time when the wards in the southern part of the prospering industrial city were being rapidly developed to meet the needs of a striving and expanding urban middle class.

Meyers High School was designed to serve the city's South Wilkes-Barre and Rolling Mill Hill neighborhoods. Its construction was part of a larger plan, developed by the Wilkes-Barre City School Board, to construct new secondary buildings in each quadrant of the city in order to meet the educational demands posed by substantial growth in Wilkes-Barre's neighborhoods during the apex of the city's population and prosperity.

The building's namesake, Dr. Elmer L. Meyers, was once a teacher at Wilkes-Barre High School. There, he created the school's first football team, literary society, and journal before leaving to attend medical school. Returning to Wilkes-Barre to practice as a physician, he was later elected to serve as school director. In that role, which he held for 25 years (from 1911 to 1936), Meyers championed the city district's school construction campaign - an effort culminating in the construction of Meyers High School.

Since its opening in 1930, Meyers has continued to serve its original function as a neighborhood public high school. Notable graduates have included Nobel Prize winning geneticist Edward Lewis; constitutional law scholar and former UC Berkeley Law School dean Jesse Choper; litigation attorney Jerome Facher; NFL wide receivers and brothers Qadry and Raghib Ismail; and film producer and "M.A.S.H." editor Stanford Tischler.

And, from the start, Meyers' auditorium has served its intended purpose as a community venue. It has hosted speakers ranging from attorney Clarence Darrow to aviator Amelia Earhart, performers such as popular violinist David Rubinoff and the Alexander Band, and countless civic events.

Meyers High School is significant as a physical manifestation of Late Progressive Era educational theory. From the rationalism of its planning, to its deliberate accommodation of industrial arts, domestic science, and physical education, to the way that it was consciously designed to function as the civic center of its urban neighborhood, it embodies the goals and aspirations of the Progressive Era in education as that movement reached its pre-Depression heights.

ELMER MEYERS HIGH SCHOOL, WILKES-BARRE, PA.

The building possesses all of the design elements desired in a high school by Progressive-Era educators: a monumental entrance; classrooms and corridors planned to accommodate the "Gary Plan" of instruction; distinct auditorium, gymnasium, science, and domestic and industrial arts wings; and didactic decorative elements (such as the auditorium's art-glass lessons in American history and civics)

It is also significant as the last major design of Robert Ireland, Wilkes-Barre's most important educational architect during the early twentieth century. Ireland, an English émigré, specialized in the design of coal breakers, factories, and other industrial structures before becoming the Wilkes-Barre School District's Supervisor of Buildings. He applied a rational, strikingly modernist ethos to the design of the city's Weaver, Palmer, and Guthrie primary schools (the latter listed individually on the National Register), and an addition to the Grant Street primary school, before authoring the city's two 1920's high schools – Grand Army of the Republic (G.A.R.) Memorial High School in the Heights section, and E.L. Meyers in South Wilkes-Barre.

Ireland's design for Meyers High School is architecturally significant as a major example of the late Beaux Arts style applied to public education, with a clever plan and monumental elevation accommodating the complex program of a large public high school to an awkward urban site and highlighting a grand auditorium and other interior spaces reflecting the building's civic purpose.

The building's heroic facade, with its colonnaded porticos, classical styling, and rational emphasis on daylighting and circulation, was specifically conceived in response to its prominent location at the intersection of two major South Wilkes-Barre thoroughfares; it is an excellent illustration of the design trends common to American public-school architecture during the early twentieth century.

At the same time, the building's straightforward details and finishes reflect Ireland's focus on efficiency, safety, and rationality – interests that were shared by Wilkes-Barre's school board and the Progressive-Era educational experts who inspired them. Inside and out, despite significant institutional neglect, the building retains significant integrity as well as all of its major character-defining features.

Elmer L. Meyers High School meets two criteria and areas of significance for the National Register of Historic Places during the period 1929 to 1952 under Criteria A and C. Under Criterion A, the building played a significant role in the history of public education in the City of Wilkes-Barre. Under Criterion C, it is not only a significant example of the monumental Beaux Arts style as applied to a late Progressive-era urban public high school, but it is also the final major work of important Wilkes-Barre architect Robert Ireland.

Larry Newman wrote the above recommendation to the State Bureau of Historic Preservation. Because he and many others in the Wilkes-Barre Area believe that Wilkes-Barre City's Meyers High School, which opened in 1930, belongs on the National Historic Registry.

Wilkes-Barre had been blessed with three well-constructed, elegantly designed high schools made of stone. They are granite and marble schools with major architectural plusses. There is perhaps more written about Elmer L. Meyers High School in this book than the other two high schools.

Coughlin for years was the oldest active high school in Pennsylvania but like all buildings "maintained" by the Wilkes-Barre Area School District, it fell into disrepair from neglect and it has been taken off-line. GAR High School was the second school in Wilkes-Barre history built by the District several years before Meyers.

Meyers is the newest of the schools and is the grandest in its unique shape and accoutrements. In its prime, Meyers hosted two swimming pools and two gymnasiums to show the care for the children of six grades 7-12 who attended the school. Graduating classes would often go back on their alumni reunion weekends to get a tour of that unique character and beauty of Meyers High School.

The same School Board that let the oldest school in Pennsylvania fall into disrepair along with other District properties permitted Meyers to go without needed maintenance for years. This book is a tale of neglect by incompetent Directors and School Officials who took schools built to last forever and declared them dead from their own neglect. It is such a sin; it will never be forgotten.

Though the Big Toxic School is being built despite its violation of EPA and DEP rules and common sense concerned citizens have joined the Save Our Schools Group, and periodically some even write an article or two in the blog or the local paper to remind others of Wilkes-Barre City's deep loss.

As discussed in both books, the board shows no respect for the beauty, strength, architecture, choice materials materials or traditions surrounding our classic schools. Meyers, for instance, had withstood systematic neglect for years, yet, the board majority shows a distinct determination to gut it for their own sordid reasons. Meyers was named to the 2018 list of at-risk Pa. structures. The district never submitted its plan for school closures or demolition to the State Bureau of Historic Preservation. Meyers belongs on the National Historic Registry. The board thinks it is the final determination on every point but the people are.

Consequently they spend a huge amount of money on a consolidated school for 4 grades, leaving the city with no high school, creating universal busing and the need for another middle school, an outdated concept that no longer works.

(And...) still more importantly, there is no support for consolidation in the educational literature of the last 50 years, much support for neighborhood schools, and evidence that consolidation harms academics, participation, security, the dropout rate AND costs more to operate.

That's all frustrating, but the board majority, the solicitor and the superintendent then outdid themselves by utilizing a building site that defies EPA and other siting guidelines, is subsidence prone, and is a coal ash dump, a potential chronic disease and cancer locus. But they obtained this non-reclaimed strip mine for a mere $4.2 million, assessed maximally at $800,000.

So, they are also bargain hunters who have used our money to reclaim a site which was the responsibility of the mining company and will be throwing more away to defray Penn Dot expenses with Cross-Valley Expressway access.

And Pagnotti, the seller, transferred their mining permit to adjacent land. Wonder what environmental boost that will provide? It's such a perfect cluster that in this county, one must at least consider...To whom does all this benefit?

Chapter 8 A Not So Great Record on Academic Achievement

The academic achievement of the Wilkes-Barre Area has been good at times and bad at times. In recent years, it has been more the latter and less of the former. When the schools were founded, the workers in the area were mostly coal miners and though they engaged in menial labor, they were nonetheless intelligent people having descended from all the nationalities who migrated from Europe in the earlier centuries. The coal mines offered a tough but a good living and the pay was good. Even today, miners make a good living with the wage coming in between $30,000 and $70,000 annually with no higher education required.

The Huber breaker, Ashely Pa.

In some places, the wages are even better. Wilkes-Barre Area Anthracite coal mining is not as prevalent today but soft coal mining jobs are plentiful in other parts of the country. For example, nine out of 10 Appalachian men do not receive college degrees; some don't even finish high school. The average starting salary for these coal mine workers is $60,000.

There are many miners, even today who can't get enough of the work in the mines. Some miners say that "craving coal dust is like nicotine: it's part of why miners love the work. "It's in the blood," said Bob Payne, 63, a retired mine worker, who says he's disappointed that his son had to quit the business after a few months because he became claustrophobic. Payne said coal mining builds "unity" and "brotherhood" among coworkers that makes working in the dark and in danger rewarding.

The safety lamp of Uncle Tony Roose, and a tribute piece
carved out of anthracite hard coal.

There was always a lot of spirit in the mines. Some old timers may remember the deep mining days in Wilkes-Barre / Scranton PA when the first block from the mine entrance was loaded with miner taverns/bars. The miners would get what they needed—a "bracer" in the form of a schnorkie at 5:00 AM or earlier to help face the day and they would get together at the same stop after work for an hour or so to get the dust out of their throats. There was a lot of collegiality.

They were proud of their children and wanted to help them do well in life. And, so, they wanted their schools to be built well and they wanted their children to be taught well and they were. Wilkes-Barre School District changed to Wilkes-Barre Area School District in 1972. Around this time the District had been at the top of its game for about 50 years. That's 50-years of high achievement.

Now, long after the days of mining in the Area, business achievement and scholastic achievement is not so good. The District took its best achievement years up front and so in the last third of the 20th century to this very day, the Wilkes-Barre Area School District has come in at about dead last in outside measurement rank. In fact, the District is almost last in the state with just one recent notable exception.

Mark Guydish, a Reporter for the Times Leader local paper wrote this about the plight of Luzerne County (Wilkes-Barre Area) schools in a short, May 2, 2018 article that fits in this chapter perfectly. Here it is:

WILKES-BARRE — Administration and school board members in the Wilkes-Barre Area School District have heard recurring complaints of low-test scores [they are true] and shoddy academic performances at schools, including frequent quotes from lists that put it on the academic slag heap of the state's 500 public districts. But they may have been handed a counterclaim Tuesday: Meyers High School made the "Niche Standout High Schools" list for 2018. In Pennsylvania, 24 high schools made the standout list. Meyers ranked 15th among those, with an overall grade of B.

No other Luzerne County schools were on the list. The "Standout" rankings start by limiting scrutiny to public high schools with at least 50 percent of students identified as economically disadvantaged. Those schools must also score an overall "Niche Grade" of B or higher — a separate "report card" letter grade devised using factors including test results, survey results, teacher salary and absenteeism, and clubs and activities, to name a few.

In naming "standout high schools," Niche uses U.S. Department of Education data, which is often several years old. In this case, most of the data is from 2014-16.

Ironically, at the same time, E.L. Meyers High School was gaining plaudits for sitting at the top of the Wilkes-Barre Area School District heap with its standout rankings, the Board Superintendent and the Board Members were busy trying to figure out a way to ram the demolition of Meyers down the throats of the neighborhood folks in South Wilkes-Barre. Here is clipping from the same time that Niche gained its records for Meyers' ranking award.

Published: 4:52 PM EDT October 18, 2016
WILKES-BARRE -- It looks as though the Wilkes-Barre Area School District wants to knock down Meyers Junior/Senior High School while still preserving parts of the building.
The school board voted Monday night in favor of a plan that would eventually demolish most of Meyers while keeping the auditorium and football field.

This is the monument to mismanagement! This historic architecturally significant neighborhood cornerstone school, that can't be replaced in its present spender and strength, is being treated as a back-yard outhouse. There needs to be a master plan to establish the most prominent use, it's value dollar wise. They started with a facility plan calling for a $13 million-dollar demolition. Then a sale, then a partial demolition; boils down to flying by the seat of their pants.

The board spends money haphazardly. It recently authorized a payment of $83,000 to relocate practice fields, yes damnit practice fields; but refused the publics request to do a $87,000 second opinion study for the historic high school, that if demolished will cost the taxpayers at least $15 million. Know what, I can't believe I just typed that last sentence.

If you were last in the state in everything, do you think you would punish the only neighborhood that brings national respect to the District? Do you think you might try to figure out what the principals and teachers of Meyers were doing differently than in the other schools? Perhaps the other schoolteachers and administrators can learn from the success of Meyers.

That would be if you cared about academic achievement and not as much about building new buildings and ripping down the most well-built buildings in the school district. How is it that the people of this area reelected most of the board that permitted the buildings to deteriorate so badly that they pleaded their case to build a new school as the only remedy. Well, obviously the Save Our Schools group led by Dr. Richard Holodick and if you asked, most of Wilkes-Barre think it is a foolhardy project that has something other than the welfare of the children at its foundation.

Let me repeat some of what we have been discussing in this chapter and at the same time perhaps repeat some of what we have already covered in this two volume set:

The Wilkes-Barre School District's high schools, Coughlin, GAR, and Meyers, even before the community mergers that occurred in the early 1970's, always had excellent academic records causing many dignitaries to visit the area. Today unfortunately, WBASD high schools are near the bottom in ranking in the state of PA. The big consolidated school approach adopted as the solution may mean the board wants to play level 6A Sports, but it also means the board is not trying to fix today's academic problems.

For example, in days gone by, the Elmer L. Meyers High School has had visits from various very famous individuals. John Philip Sousa performed in its magnificent auditorium on August 31, 1931. Amelia Earhart visited in spring of 1936 after the Meyer's High School Women's Club brought her in to talk to students about "Adventures in Flying".

More recently, but not consistently, the Meyers school had Travis Clark and Hunter Thomsen from *We The Kings* perform an acoustic set in October 2009. After winning the High School Hookup V2.0 from local radio station 97 BHT, the two members performed a free show in the auditorium.

For many years, all three high schools have offered and still offer sports in the Fall, Winter, and Spring that are open for all students to join and compete. Those sports include cheerleading, cross country, field hockey, football, golf, boys' and girls' soccer, girls' volleyball, boys' and girls' basketball, swimming & diving, wrestling, baseball, softball, and track & field. No student is left without an activity.

The district's schools offer year-round clubs that students can sign up and participate in. The clubs offered range from High School specific clubs, such as the Elmprint Club and Colophon Club, to national clubs and organizations, such as F.B.L.A. and National Honors Society.

Meyers, for example, offers two clubs dedicated to publishing the school newspaper, Elmprint, and producing the yearbook, Colophon. Other clubs offered include the Art Club, Chess Club, Computer Club, Diversity Club, Drama Club, Envirothon, F.B.L.A., Key Club, Math Club, National Honors Society, Scholastic Scrimmage, Ski Club, Spanish Club, Speech and Debate, Stage Crew, Student Council, and Watershed Project.

In terms of musical groups, the schools offer chorus, jazz band, marching band, and orchestra.

Led by Attorneys Kim and Ruth Borland, and supported by many, including the late Steve Bollinger of Phillies Phinest, the E. L.

Meyers High School is known across the country for its speech and debate team. Founded in 1997, Meyers hosts the Martin Luther King Open Speech and Debate Tournament every January. The team was tied for a national championship with four other schools in 2009 at the National Catholic Forensic League championships held in Albany, New York. The Borland's, like many others in the community favor neighborhood schools.

The team offers students a host of events to choose to compete in. Some of the events that the team hosts include Lincoln–Douglas debate, policy debate, public forum debate, extemporaneous speaking, declamation, oral interpretation, original oratory, duo interpretation of literature, and dramatic interpretation.

Notable Coughlin alumni include the following plus a number of others as this list is incomplete:

- Dorothy Andrews Elston Kabis, 33rd Treasurer of the United States
- Jeff Cardoni, composer of American Pie Presents: The Naked Mile, Open Season 3, and CSI: Miami (since 2002);
- Catherine Chandler, poet;
- Pat Finn, host of The Joker's Wild from 1990–91 and Shop 'til You Drop (1991–94; 1996–98; 2000-2);
- Ham Fisher (1918), cartoonist of Joe Palooka comic strip.
- James Karen, actor.
- Bruce Kozerski, former American football center in the National Football League for the Cincinnati Bengals
- Ron Solt, former American football guard in the National Football League for the Indianapolis Colts and the Philadelphia Eagles
- Harold Rainsford Stark (1940), U.S. Navy Admiral; Chief of Naval Operations (1939–42).
- James L. Nelligan, Former Congressman from Pennsylvania's 11th Congressional District (1981-1983)

Notable G.A.R. alumni include the following plus a number of others as this list is also incomplete:

- David Bohm - Quantum physicist who was involved in the Manhattan Project.[citation needed]
- Mark James Klepaski- Bass player for the rock band Breaking Benjamin.
- Greg Skrepenak- Former NFL player and former Luzerne County Commissioner.
- Sam Savitt - Author and illustrator, official artist of the U.S. Equestrian Team.[20]
- Bob Sura- NBA player who last played for the Houston Rockets
- Robert Williams - Quarterback for Notre Dame, 1956–1958
- Maurice Peoples - Olympic sprinter, 1972
- Mark Glowinski - NFL player for the Indianapolis Colts.
- Notable Meyers alumni include the following plus a number of others as this list is incomplete:
- Qadry Ismail – NFL Analyst, Former NFL wide receiver
- Raghib Ismail – Former NFL wide receiver
- Phil Ostrowski – NFL player
- Dan Chariton – Screenwriter

Edward B. Lewis – Geneticist, Nobel Prize Winner (1995)

Chapter 9 The Big Toxic School on Contaminated Land—On Its Way

40 yr. school? Looks like a Plasticville Model from the outside right side of montage

The Consolidation from the City's Three High Schools

When the consolidated / combined high school opens in Plains Township, the plan is that this huge complex nicknamed The Big Toxic School will replace a fantastic trio of historic, well-built, but aging buildings. The newest of these will have passed its 90th anniversary. Of course, the original Coughlin Wilkes-Barre High Building is over 110 years old.

This new consolidated mega school facility is expected by the current board to continue to serve the towns that joined with the city to form the Wilkes-Barre Area School District in the 1960s, giving up their own high schools in the process.

It is a safe bet that none of the current officials will be in office if something happens and the new school does not make it to its expected 40-year anniversary. With the debt on the taxpayers from The Big Toxic School if its lifetime ends at 30 years instead of 40 years, the taxpayers will be paying for two monstrosities at a time.

A big factor relating to paying off the debt from the Toxic High & the Toxic land will be enrollment. Will the public enroll their children in what many believe to be an unsafe school. If the present trend of students leaving for charter and cyber schools which is now the highest in the state at 600, a 60% to 70% enrollment will not provide the reimbursement from the state to pay the debt service. Then what?

The Save Our Schools mantra will never look so smart. Then again if the DEP or the EPA shuts the school down after one year of toxic fumes and polluted water run-off, who pays for it all then? The impoverished taxpayers of Wilkes-Barre Area will be paying while the new board is scurrying to figure out how to repair Coughlin, GAR and Meyers again as permanent schools. We kid you not.

There will be a new name, new colors, a new mascot and a new alma mater. But the story, as it did when that first high school opened its doors in 1867, will go on unless it is stopped.

The groundbreaking for the new complex was held in April 2020. One of your authors' Brian Kelly was there to check it out. Of course he was just an observer with no speaking role. Kelly lined up with the protesters. Yes, there were some protestors who showed up at the event and Kelly was very pleased to have been one of them. This was the formal groundbreaking for Wilkes-Barre Area School district's new consolidated high school.

Groundbreaking Ceremony for Wilkes-Barre Area High School

WNEP News sent Jessica Albert to cover the April 12, 2020 event, which was held on a Friday Morning. The dozen or so protestors that showed up at the ceremony, were mostly from the Save our Schools organization. They had previously made known their concerns, being worried that the land the school is being built on could be harmful to students' health. Would you want your child to breathe air from a school built over a toxic mine site?

The Cross-Valley Expressway, shown to the right, grey looking like a moon shot is the 78 acres of coal ash, culm. Note all surrounding areas are green. With the exception of to the left of the cross valley is the beginning of more gray, a Pagnotti property.

The site is on nearly 80 acres of old strip and deep mined mining land, prone to subsidence, that will be the location of Wilkes-Barre Area School district's new consolidated high school.

"It's just something that we've been striving for. We believe our students deserve something like this, our community deserves something like this," said Wilkes-Barre Area Superintendent Brian Costello.

The new school will combine the district's three high schools into one. It's a project that has been controversial among some parents and several of them showed up to the groundbreaking to protest. They believe the land is not safe for students because it used to be a toxic mine and a dump.

It's very concerning," said parent Lois Grimm. "You wouldn't even be able to build a house on this property because of the levels that they found in the soil but we're putting a school on it. I mean, that right there should give the school board members pause." But the school board members have their own reasons, which they have not revealed.

WNEP TV reporters spoke with a representative from the DEP who say the land is safe to build on. That gives you an idea of how deep this conspiracy to defraud the people is. "I think the school district has identified the site. They've studied it. They know what contamination is here and they have appropriate measures to deal with it to make it safe for reuse for a school," said DEP official Michael Bedrin. Ask Bedrin if he would send his children to the Big Toxic School.

And, so there we have it, the portrayal of the 100-year academic history of the Wilkes-Barre School District, continued past 1972 when additional communities were brought in. During this period, the outstanding curriculum was way ahead of its time as the historic high schools delivered high quality education. That is now a vestige of the past.

Summary

The coal miners took raw pride in their educational system and they funded it to be excellent in its academic achievement—and for years, it was. But it is no longer. WBASD is a bottom dweller in the states' ranking where the miners always assured top level academic achievement.

We can know how great it was by studying the depth of the damage over at least the last 50 years. Both the academic curriculum and the facilities have been grossly neglected. The Board's official priorities during this period switched from the best in academics by not designing a curriculum to meet the demographics of the students enrolled. Instead, the emphasis became sports and the dollars reflect the new concentration of effort. This final straw is the Taj Mahal toxic mine shaft high shifting its emphasis from academia to sports. This has taken a toll in just the first year playing as a jointure.

It is proven and proven again in WBASD, that less students have the opportunity to participate in sports in monster schools. Fewer athletes competed in varsity fall sports for the new Wilkes-Barre Area Wolfpack when compared to the 2018-19 rosters of the three city high schools whose programs were consolidated this year, but school officials say the merger made more programs available for all students. More programs but less participants mean more kids on the bench if they choose to play at all. No thank you.

Football roster totals in the final year of the three separate schools, according to figures provided by Wilkes-Barre Area athletic director Michael Namey to the local papers, showed 28 Coughlin, 38 Meyers and 23 GAR players (89 total). Boys soccer teams, meanwhile, had 30, 22 and 14 players at those respective schools (66 total). Mr. Namey said to the board in a public board meeting, "The consolidation of sports gives more students the opportunity to participate." Your authors sure hope he doesn't teach math.

Chapter 10 Did WBASD Blow Its Budget?

Budget Financial Failures

It is vital to the district's 7000 students, the taxpayers and especially senior citizens who are scraping to get along, to "hold elected officials accountable." The belief of Save Our (neighborhood) Schools is that the education of all students is vital to our community. Neighborhood schools are vital to our City; the quality of education and financial stability of the district. safe/quality facilities and the aforementioned notions are fundamental to our citizens.

All the people of the Wilkes-Barre Area together need to hold elected officials accountable for poor academic achievement and a lot of wasted money. First of all we find a deplorable student statewide ranking:443 out of 501. Secondly the board wastes money like a drunken sailor. We have cited the $ six million spent with nothing physical to show for it, and a potential deficit of $29 million dollars, without required construction; the destruction of historic "built to last forever" high schools due to neglect; the need to raise taxes to the max allowed by law just to cover errors and omissions.

The following are derived from the mandated state audit. It is not a very responsible picture for a board about to enter a building/renovation project that could exceed a HALF BILLION DOLLARS. This concern is compounded by the dire fact that district's citizens are at the poverty level. Annual average salaries at $38,000 and a major aging population whose only income is social security. If we couple this with the district spending a quarter of a BILLION on less than a third of their students, with two thirds of the elementary students attending school in 5 aged facilities. What has this board done right?

And the biggie you ask? This outrageous expenditure does not address the district's major problems, academic failures, fleeing students, with the highest truancy rate in the state. This board does not cut the resident taxpayers a break and they should not be cut a break for their poor management of the district. After all, it is their job.

Excerpts from State Audit

In order to assess the District's financial stability, we reviewed several financial benchmarks to evaluate changes in its financial position over a period of four fiscal years beginning July 1, 2011 through the year ending June 30, 2015. We found that the District is in a declining financial position. Our discussion of the District's declining financial position will cover the following areas:

- General Fund Balance
- Budgetary Operational Deficits
- Operating Position
- Budgeted vs. Actual Expenditures and Revenues

In addition, we found that the District's administration failed to submit and the Board failed to require monthly treasurer's reports for the Board's review and approval from December 2013 to December 2014. In addition, we found that the majority of the treasurer's reports that the Board did receive during the audit period were incomplete and untimely. The lack of complete and timely treasurer's reports limits the Board's ability to make informed financial decisions.

General Fund Balance: The General Fund balance decreased from $16.8 million on July 1, 2012 to $6.7 million on June 30, 2015. The decrease during the 2014-15 fiscal year was over $6.7 million.

We have concerns that the board does not provide adequate information about its activities. In fact, sometimes it provides no information on very costly board actions. A prime example was having a completely designed two high school consolidation and under new business, near the end of the meeting a motion was made and passed to add the students from the third high school to the new school. At this time, there were no change order costs, no additional construction cost to increase the size of the building; and no chance for the public to comment. Nonetheless the motion passed. Where's the beef?

The auditor's state, "The lack of complete and timely treasurer's reports limits the board's ability to make informed decisions." That's all the Auditor General could come up with? Who is he related to was a deep concern after that report.

The General Fund balance is a necessary component of a fiscally healthy district. Just as individuals should maintain a savings account to deal with emergencies or other unforeseen events, districts should also have funds in reserve to pay for emergency repairs or interruptions to revenues. A decreasing fund balance also reduces the District's ability to generate investment income.

We identified three areas which contributed to the decreasing General Fund balance:

- Budgeted expenditures exceeded budgeted revenues (budgetary deficit) for the 2011-12, 2012-13, 2013-14, and 2014-15 fiscal years.

- Actual expenditures exceeded actual revenues (operating deficit) for the 2012-13, 2013-14, and 2014-15 fiscal years.

- Actual expenditures exceeded budgeted expenditures for the 2013-14 and 2014-15 fiscal years.

Table 2

Wilkes-Barre Area SD: Comparison of Operating Position			
Fiscal Year Ending June 30	Total Revenues and Other Financing Sources	Total Expenditures and Other Uses	(Deficit)
2013	$98,894,946	$99,254,021	$(359,075)
2014	$100,399,769	$103,445,532	$(3,045,763)
2015	$104,762,179	$111,501,133	$(6,738,954)
Total	$304,056,894	$314,200,687	$(10,143,792)

Budgeted vs. Actual Expenditures and Revenues: As shown in Table 3 below, the District's actual expenditures exceeded its board approved budgeted expenditures in both the 2013-14 and 2014-15 fiscal years. Exceeding budgetary expenditures is a violation of Section 609 of the Public School Code.

Table 3

Wilkes-Barre Area SD: Comparison of Budget vs. Actual Expenditures			
Fiscal Year Ending June 30	Budgeted Amount	Actual Amount	(Over) Budget
2014	$101,858,700	$103,398,165	$(1,539,465)
2015	$111,076,875	$111,501,133	$(424,258)
Total	$212,935,575	$214,899,298	$(1,963,723)

As stated between table 2 & 3, "Exceeding budgetary expenditures is a violation of section 609 of the public-school code." But then again so is segregating the high school with the highest percentage of minorities; but that's federal. Or purchasing un-reclaimed mine land, state violation; begin site work costing over a million prior to owning the property.

How confident are you that this is the best way to govern school districts? Do you trust this board to manage a HALF BILLION DOLLAR PROJECT?

Yes, the district has been underfunded by the state, all the more reason to handle the funds you do have vigilantly. This impoverished City is on the re-bound with center city, the colleges and universities, riverfront, and sports/entertainment. Desperately needed is the restoration of our neighborhoods. The Wilkes University study pointing to the growing neighborhood blight and number of family residents' homes for sale are vivid examples that the neighborhoods are heading in a reverse direction. We truly believe that the restoration of the neighborhood schools will be the needed beginning of bringing the neighborhoods back to what they once were. What is your opinion?

Parent comment at a recent board meeting:

Several other comments levied by citizens over the decision to consolidate and build the boondoggle school over a tox mine dump: There will be no tax base any longer in Wilkes Barre= no money for the school districts. It's a matter of financial survival. Don't these people realize you can't get blood from a stone? Caused by the cost of teacher pensions, which need to be re-structured, etc..

In a poverty level district not doing due diligence to utilize existing facilities, no less historic facilities with a potential forever shelf life could easily run the district into educational and financial bankruptcy. The development of a plan to submit to the Pa. Department of Education that segregated the high school with the highest percentage of minorities and economically disadvantaged students constituted possible malfeasance in a public office.
The plan to build a consolidated school for 200 students on 2.7 acres, pictured on a prior page, 35 acres recommended, downtown on a one-way narrow street; forbidden by zoning, and not waiting for zoning waivers cost the taxpayers $6 million. This board treats taxpayer dollars like it owns a goose that produces golden eggs.

Chapter 11 Success Begins with Planning

If the School District's Building Assets, which by nature of their jobs, the Board and the Superintendent have sworn to care for, protect from harm, and maintain in top shape, were a human body , a look at the Act 34 report of deficiencies would cause one to conclude that the study is over. There is no need to go on. The patient has died and it died a long time ago.

Yes, ladies and gentlemen, that is how poorly the caretakers of the WBASD building properties have done their job.

The beginning of this chapter is taken from the following report:

ACT 34 HEARING BOOKLET
Wilkes-Barre Area School District 730 South Main Street,
Wilkes-Barre, PA 18702
Concerning the construction of a New High School
Date: October 29, 2018
Time: 6:00 P.M.
Location: Cafeteria Leo E. Solomon - Plains Memorial Junior High School
43 Abbott Street Plains Township, PA 18705

The purpose of the Act 34 Hearing was to present and discuss all aspects concerning the construction of a New High School. This snippet concentrates on the deficiencies at Meyers and GAR High Schools. One would conclude that Coughlin is in worse shape as the WBASB has since decommissioned that school.

EDUCATIONAL NEED FOR THE PROJECT

Background:

Other than the renovations to the Edward Mackin school in 2016, the District has not had a new building, or a major renovation project completed in the District since the Leo E. Solomon-Plains Memorial Elementary and Junior High School project was completed in 1996.

Thus, the average age of the district's facilities is 65 years. The district currently operates five (5) K-6 elementary schools, one (1) 7-8 middle school, two (2) 7-12 Jr./Sr. High Schools, one (1) 9-10 high school, and one (1) 9-12 high school. A summary of the District's buildings is recited on a document called PlanCon A09, which can be researched and found readily.

Other than the Edward Mackin School, all the remaining buildings need repairs and renovations to upgrade the facilities to current standards for continued use. Code deficiencies and accessibility compliance issues exist throughout the district's buildings. Many schools have undersized classrooms aka overcrowded classrooms.

The buildings are hindered by insufficient electrical and data systems; have insufficient mechanical systems and are not handicapped accessible. In addition, the schools do not provide adequate space and space relationships to meet contemporary educational standards or the District's educational programming requirements.

Enrollment Growth:

The average current size for each grade level ranges from 508 to 566 students with an average of 531 students per grade. Between 2019 and 2026 the Pennsylvania Department of Education (PDE) projections indicate a 7.8% increase in enrollment in grades 9-12. PDE enrollment projections for the Wilkes-Barre Area School District are reproduced in Table 3.1 in the report. The projections are based on actual enrollments for December 2016. Projections through 2025-2026 are also listed.

District administration and personnel have indicated that, in general, they feel the district's enrollment is growing. Interviews with district administration and personnel revealed a consensus that the PDE enrollment projections appear likely to occur.

District board and administration have indicated that the current school facilities are inadequate to accommodate the projected growth and that the project should provide a design capacity for the current average enrollment per grade level plus an amount for growth.

Current Building Conditions:

Without some repair and some renovation, the existing high school facilities have significant building deficiencies that make it difficult for the buildings to support the district's educational program. James M. Coughlin High School was closed due to safety issues and code deficiencies. Elmer L. Meyers Jr./Sr. High School and G.A.R. Jr./Sr. High School have some systems that fail to comply with current codes and are energy inefficient. Meyers, in particular, has building systems that have exceeded expected life expectancies, would be expensive to replace, and are obsolete. These are things that should have been addressed previously by the board but over the years, they were neglected by plan and never budgeted.

A summary of the deficiencies follows. Please refer to the feasibility study for a comprehensive summary of building deficiencies.

Elmer L. Meyers Junior/Senior High School:

The building continues to serve grades 7-12 through an expensive on-going maintenance program. In recent years, areas of the roof and portions of the water supply system to the building have been replaced; however, the building has not had significant renovations since it was originally constructed. The building in its current configuration does not accommodate the district's educational program. Classrooms are undersized, toilet facilities are inadequate, and accessibility standards are not compliant with code. The district's educational programs cannot be accommodated without significant renovations to the space that would impact structural systems.

If as much time was spent over the years by the Board, fixing problems at Meyers as they occurred, the time it took to retro-create this list could have all been saved. The maintenance philosophy of the board can be summarized in one word: N-E-G-L-E-C-T

G.A.R. Junior/Senior High School:

The building continues to serve grades 7-12 through an expensive on-going maintenance program. In recent years portions of the mechanical HVAC system have been replaced; however, the building has not had comprehensive renovations in several decades.

If as much time was spent over the years by the Board, fixing problems at GAR as they occurred, the time it took to retro-create this list could have all been saved. The maintenance philosophy of the board can be summarized in that same one word: N-E-G-L-E-C-T.

A similar document could be produced for Coughlin but the WBASB has already thrown in the towel on the City's first high school.

District Recommendations:

Based on the building deficiencies, the inability of the buildings to adequately accommodate the District's educational program and the District's enrollment growth, and in consideration of the District's finances, the District intends to construct a new consolidated high school for the District's 9-12 student population.

District Administration directed the Architect to assist the District with developing a space program. The program incorporates the District's space needs into the new facility. The Program is based on the District's curriculum goals over the next ten to twenty years. District administration considered the current and projected enrollment; its educational programs' objectives; the number, grouping, and nature of the students enrolled in the facility; spatial relationships within the facility and surrounding site; interrelationships between various programs and activities; technological advances; and other provisions that would improve the learning environment and promote educational effectiveness and staff efficiency.

The population of Wilkes-Barre Area openly wonders why we should trust the current board of directors and the Superintendent to take care of a project with a cost from $121 Million to A Half Billion Dollars over forty years. New construction is not as durable and will not have the shelf life of the schools that have given their 90 to 110 years of their forever lives serving the district.

Chapter 12 A Maintenance Model for The WBASD

Please don't forget that first and foremost nearly all evidence says don't consolidate schools because it harms academics, student sense of well-being, student participation, and that it increases costs. Having said that, the site is receiving such attention because outside of perhaps Chernobyl, it would be difficult to find a worse spot to build a school.

How All School Buildings Should Be Maintained.

Wilkes-Barre High School – later Coughlin –
A one-time handsome building

Later circa 1950, the Coughlin Annex was built to its left.

In 2017 the school was closed and a big ugly fence built in front of it. This building can be restored and History would love it. My dad went to this school. Graduated Circa 1933

By the way, looking at the Coughlin building today, you can tell there has been no building maintenance plan whatsoever ever for Wilkes-Barre Area School District. And, that is not funny and has never been funny! That's why this book is needed. No consolidated school or any other school new would be needed if the board had prudently executed an approved building maintenance program for all three city-based high schools. Maintenance was not on their agenda. But, neglect was.

Neglect creates a need to scrap the dilapidated buildings left in the wake of bad policies that produce inevitable results. Nobody thinks building a new school is a good idea if schools are maintained. Worse than that is the decision to build a Big Toxic School on top of a poisonous chemical coal ash laden mine dump. Who was the board kidding?

Here it is on the left in its patented school board ugly filthy early scaffold regalia. Picture is by Kathleen Kelly, Brian's daughter.

There is no maintenance plan and there never was in the Wilkes-Barre Area School District. It is hard to believe. That is the cause of so many school buildings being in a dilapidated state. With a plan, all buildings would be in ship shape today and there would be no need for building a new school anywhere, especially not over a toxic mine shaft.

Think about what happened. A board that was derelict in its duty somehow got rewarded with a new school and the taxpayers got punished for not firing the same board multiple times when it had the opportunity in past elections.

Is Good Maintenance an Essential Need?

Absolutely yes!

Well operated school districts operate with a maintenance plan so that district buildings last as long as possible and they do not have to be replaced prematurely.

The fact is that without a reliable and routine planned maintenance program and a scheduled preventive maintenance plan, a school district cannot effectively maintain its facilities. The Wilkes-Barre Area School District can serve as the "poster child" for what happens when there is no policy other than neglect. The Wilkes-Barre School

Board can swear truthfully that neglect does not work even if that is all you have.

A top-flight program cannot be a short-term commitment. Instead, it must be an ongoing continued work task, assessment of conditions, and the development and implementation of preventive and corrective measures. The results of such a program can affect the district's facilities by a reduction of overall costs, lessening any negative impact on the educational process, providing stable conditions, adding increased years of reliable service, and giving the school district the ability to adequately budget.
The advantages add up as students get a non-disruptive education and the district is never surprised by facilities down situations that cost many dollars to bring back on-line.

Communication:

Having a well-oiled maintenance plan helps all aspects of the district. The prime uses of such a program /plan are the development of adequate communication to assess each school and the condition of facilities on an ongoing basis. If the district officials are not checking the condition of the buildings regularly, how can they determine what is needed to keep them properly functioning? How will they know when to maintain any new refurbishments or new construction? They can't! It is impossible

A well-developed program brings the schools' staffs and the districts' maintenance department together to find and resolve maintenance concerns and to have a record of what has happened and needs to happen to make things better. It is very important that ongoing schools' staff and new employees understand how the system works and what part they play in its continuing operations.

Exceptional:

Those in the WBASD understand that many schools are unique, and they are exceptional from other building types since they encounter intense use because of the daily use and abuse of young occupants. The "kids" do not necessarily care how they treat district assets. Thus, the schools deserve special design requirements and special monitoring. With such high human traffic in schools, there is more of a need for facilities to be always up than in a typical business.

Consequently, rigid standards and extra precautions are required to be taken to ensure life, safety, and building continuance. All buildings are seasonal but with long periods of use and short periods of limited occupancy though exceptions always do occur—and at the worst times—backup plans are even more important.

All of these factors make school maintenance difficult to accomplish without interfering with the educational process and therefore lengthy maintenance tasks must often be done after school hours or during vacations periods.

Districts that ignore these requirements end up like the Wilkes-Barre Area School District. Over time, school buildings become so out-of-repair that they need to be replaced as the neglect catches up with what a normal maintenance plan would provide. Simple repairs that are ignored can add up to a school needing to be replaced because of official negligence, which is often called deferred maintenance. What actually happens is that the deferral of maintenance becomes permanent until a big issue arises unexpectedly and then all the resources are needed to address it.

Training and Development

No employee or supervisor seems to know anything about construction or building maintenance at the Wilkes-Barre Area School District. There are no architects or engineers on staff. Therefore, any consultant can use the buzz words of the trade to get the best of a superintendent or a custodian with whom they work.

The WBA board for years has opted to "get by" without the right team of knowledgeable experts and craftsmen. The fact is a district such as ours with over $300 million in real estate assets needs to be led by skilled professionals such as a school district architect and / or a competent engineer. This is just the first phase of assuring building assets last for their entire expected life. Getting all you can out of building assets saves the most money for the taxpayers. Replacing poorly maintained assets with new buildings is the costliest alternative to doing it right.

Consequently, in most school districts other than the WBASD, building maintenance has grown to become a sophisticated process with new equipment, materials, and maintenance personnel required to have more technical skills to keep the major systems -- electrical, mechanical, and special systems in operation. To do this, nothing happens overnight. Instead, formal career path training must be offered, and motivated individuals must be selected, and the selected individuals must attend courses to increase their skills. Our district does not believe in educating its own staff. Instead it hires contractors who answer to the academic superintendent of schools, who is also untrained in building matters.

Continual education on the latest and evolving technical building issues is a base requirement. A district that uses its skilled academic personnel including its Superintendent to perform such maintenance work is doomed to failure in both the academic side and the facilities side. Wilkes-Barre needs to renovate almost all its buildings and its academic achievement is among the worst in the state. I just proved my point. It's like lighting a candle at both ends. It only seems brighter for a short while before it burns you and the limited light ends.

One of this board's greatest faults is that when they took the oath to serve the people of WBASD, they promised to care for the $300 million in district building assets. However, they were either kidding or they reneged on their oath and instead neglected all maintenance.

When the buildings began to crumble as expected, pretending it was not because of them, they cried for help from the people to bail them out. The people are out of money folks! It is hard to believe that this same untrustworthy board want the people to trust them again with a new building expected to cost a HALF BILLION over 40 years. They hope to build something new—which of course will also have no maintenance plan for reaching its expected life. Yes, it is a shame. It is a big sin but the board thinks they run the people and not vice versa.

The fact is this is the way this board operates. It would not change if we gave them a down payment of $121 million for the new project. What would happen? In 25 years, the new Lionel Plasticville Big

Toxic School a like everything else this board touches, will need replacing. The Board thinks the taxpaying residents are all dummies. We are for sure if we do not watch everything they do and hold them accountable for all the cost overruns noted in this report. There will be many more if the public permits.

As noted, the board does not believe in a maintenance plan so they never created one—even for the new school. Ask them about that please before you ever vote for any one of them again. It is hard to imagine until you see Coughlin and Meyers after their neglect.

There was no plan and there still is no maintenance plan. Moreover, there is no plan for the new building. If anything, ever gets fixed today in the Wilkes-Barre Area School District, it is not part of an overall plan. It may not be an accident but it sure is not part of a major plan that a competent, prudent board would have been created to assure buildings last a long time—at least to the end of their estimated lives.

Historically, our school district acts only when necessary and never by plan. As witnessed recently with Mackin School, Meyers, and Coughlin, nothing happens until the disrepair reaches a point where a major renovation or a replacement project is the only option. Based on what you know, would you hire anybody from the WBASB to make sure your house is kept in good repair. We know that answer because we are smarter than this board thinks.

Think about your own home for a minute. Say your only toilet breaks. When this happens, you fix it or have it fixed post haste. When your roof has a leak, you fix it. When the porch has a rotted plank, you fix it. When there is a hole in the plaster or sheet-rock wall, you fix it. You do not wait until you have to replace the whole house after ignoring small repairs brings your home to a beyond repair condition.

Ask yourself: why should citizens of WBASD trust this board with new property worth well in excess of $100 million when we would not trust them with the upkeep of our own $80,000 +- domicile? . The principles are the same. This board fails on the simple things – things that the people would do well.

The school board for many, many years chose to operate without an appropriate qualified maintenance staff headed by somebody who understands all aspects of the building trades. I am talking about a competent architect or engineer such as those employed by Scranton University or Misericordia University and the other colleges in this area. The school superintendent, though perhaps a gritty and feisty administrator is not competent in the trades, nor should he or she have to be competent in the skills of building and grounds maintenance.

With our school district last in academic achievement testing in the state, perhaps this superintendent is not competent enough to even oversee academic achievement. Or perhaps his avocation of controlling the maintenance and construction of new district assets is keeping him from his primary duty of maintaining a high academic rating as when Dr. Jeff Namey were in his position?

From all observations of the WBASB, the Superintendent himself uses his cronies in the trades industry without first having negotiated long-term maintenance contracts to solve issues as they arise. Whether plumbing, carpentry, electrical or other emergencies that the custodial staff is not prepared to handle, the superintendent is forced to get involved to contract with a favored cadre of cronies or perhaps relatives to get a problem resolved. Otherwise, the problem will be neglected, get worse, and be unsolved and be more serious when the next emergency comes around. That is clearly a recipe for building new buildings after the older versions are permitted to fritter away. We've seen it happen.

Since calling in outside help, even if part of a friend or crony team, puts stress on the repair budget (if there is one), it is likely that the Superintendent might choose to postpone actual repairs. The Wilkes-Barre Area Super uses that approach. More than likely, like, me, you have gone into a district school, and found a sign on the restroom door asking you to find another toilet someplace else in the building. It is a common occurrence.

A sign can be reused and is lots cheaper than fixing a problem when it occurs. I bet you have found signs calling out other issues and perhaps dangers in our schools. The worse than ugly cheap particle board imitation wood scaffolding outside several school buildings stands as a witness to the lack of care provided by the board to such buildings Signs are cheaper than repairs but using signs v repairs is not a good building maintenance practice.

From this   to this

Cost $243,000

Front entrance particle board and PVC mirror the same look at the side entrance of Meyers You might have gone into Meyers High School for example. See above. Over the last several years this was the look and it was underneath a maze of particle board built to protect passersby from falling building material. Yet, nothing is ever on the top of the scaffold—not even a pebble. Does that mean the scaffolding is some kind of ruse?

For a school board hell-bent on making Meyers look like a school needing to be torn down, adorning the entrances with cheap blue painted particle board surely does the trick. The intricate PVC pipe maze adds an additional aura of incompetence to the overall picture of the front of what otherwise would be a beautiful school entrance. The temporary fix must have become permanent recently but it sure is ugly. AND the taxpayers' paid over a QUARTER OF A MILLION DOLLARS!

If the board wants Meyers to look bad, shoddy work like this is a sure way to do it. It makes the school look to be in worse shape than it really is. It is the product of a patchwork quilt maintenance philosophy that no competent craftsmen would recommend.

Why would the superintendent spend the money to fix something needing the proper expertise—such as say a plumbing issue, when he or she has a private Water Closet tucked handily away in his or her own comfortable and private office. Besides there is more dollars ;eft for the sports program.

The point in this chapter is simply that without a well-conceived, written maintenance plan available, nobody can ascertain problems of any nature. How could they ever be fixed with no system in place. We have demonstrated that the Wilkes-Barre Area School District uses *neglect* as its only maintenance philosophy. That is quite obvious.

This is how buildings, including school buildings, without a plan for their ongoing regular maintenance eventually fall into a state of complete disrepair and begin to look so shabby that inspectors might suggest ripping them down and building new buildings rather than investing in significant repair work.

Toilets are a good example of which we can all relate. Neglect causes one broken toilet on one floor to become two broken toilets on two floors until there is only one functional toilet left in a building. Then what? Well, then the wise men in charge declare the problem unsolvable and decide to move all school operations to another building with functional latrines.

Whether the issue is broken toilets, weak beams, leaky roofs, falling plaster, exposed asbestos, or missing floor sections, eventually, the list of to-be-fixed items becomes so great that the Board Superintendent decides to punt rather than deal with an area outside his or her expertise. Punting is a regular occurrence in the Superintendent's office play book.

In school districts that have spent the time to construct a maintenance plan and have hired an in-house staff with expertise to use the preventive maintenance plan, as a rule, holes do not appear in floors and toilets do not break all of a sudden. Instead, buildings last and do not need replacing after a few maintenance incidents.

Deferred repairs quickly can turn into replacement events. Colleges with many buildings on campus have the same issues as school districts. Stanford University recently published a report titled "Guidelines for Life Cycle Cost Analysis," which explains how as a building or campus ages, the cumulative cost of operating and maintaining facilities significantly impacts the overall budget — not just the maintenance budget.

Even when funds are set aside to construct new buildings, they rarely extend to the ongoing operational costs vital to maintaining the facility and slowing the decline of building utility and performance.

In other words, deferred maintenance is a sure way of increasing long-term building costs. The best approach is to fix it before it is broken through a preventive maintenance program. But, you need a team of artisans to do that. The team costs lots less in the long run, however, than not having the team.

The greater issue with deferred maintenance is that it grows in scope — and cost — the longer it is prolonged. Don't put off 'til tomorrow what you can do today. This is a lesson still unlearned by the Wilkes-Barre Area School Board (WBASB).

When a repair is delayed, it is still subject to the daily use and abuse of school occupants. Students do not stop coming to school because a toilet is down or a light is out or a floor is overly slippery. In fact, it's not uncommon for a "repair" to turn into a "replacement" because, in the process of being deferred, it becomes completely broken.

Replacing a door, lock, window, etc., is much more costly than simply repairing it in a timely manner. But not only is the expense higher, there is also a frequently overlooked cost in staff productivity as replacements typically take much longer to complete than repairs.

When whole buildings need to be replaced because of excessive neglect, the costs grow out of the affordability range of most taxpayer bases. Sometimes a School Board chooses not to take the resources of the taxpayers into consideration as is the case with WBASB.

On the other hand, buildings and facilities that have implemented comprehensive preventive maintenance programs have found that the operation of their systems is more reliable, and those systems also last longer and cost less in the long run.

Preventative maintenance measures

Projects that are put on hold, repair that is neglected, or maintenance that is ignored add up to a costly and complex problem. The cost of deferred maintenance could potentially be 30 times that of the early intervention cost. From what we have seen with the notion of a new consolidated high school in Plains Twp., there is still no overall plan nor a preventive maintenance plan in place and unless it is a secret, the board has not discussed increases in the quality and quantity of maintenance personnel even with a new building in the on-deck circle.

In WBASD, there are no architects or engineers in the hiring pipeline to make sure construction and maintenance is performed safely and appropriately. The youthful Superintendent appears to be the only one checking out the construction site. And, that is not good. When the Superintendent is in the field checking construction, is someone from the custodial staff doing his Superintendent job?

And, so, what can we expect long after the current board is out of office say in twenty or thirty years? God forbid! Will their new consolidated Taj Mahal on a mine shaft be ready to be replaced because with no assigned maintenance personnel and no plan, it will have been neglected?

For the current board it may not even matter. None of them will be around for the folks of 2050 to blame for their continued imprudent maintenance philosophy. This board has no plans to make maintenance better so they must be fired. It is that simple. We fire school boards simply by electing alternative members. It really is that easy. Then we make sure they are doing their jobs. We have learned that is not a given.

What we are saying is that the importance of preventative maintenance cannot be overstated. If this current board were better caretakers of the real estate assets of the District, there would be no need for a major repair project and certainly no need for a huge high school consolidation project designed to bankrupt a community.

Experts estimate that between two and six percent of an annual operating budget should be spent on preventative maintenance in order to effectively minimize a facility's rate of decay. Quality building materials such as granite as was used in proper high school buildings before 1950, is hard to come by within budget but the buildings would surely last longer with top-grade materials. Besides materials, prevention not only saves money, but it helps facilities avoid replacement — which requires capital assets and often creates an extensive process from evaluation and design to funding and implementation.

By nature, preventive maintenance is the least disruptive, singular in resolution, planned for in advance alternative and often includes training for future maintenance. Most of all, it helps reduce building failure and poor conditions that can negatively impact mission critical building operations, a school district's image, student results and retention, energy efficiency and even employee morale.

Nobody would expect a school district to operate without a boss. In other words, it goes without saying that a person schooled in curricula and the proper ways of running a school's academic programs, most often called a principal or a superintendent is an obvious necessity in order to operate a school. A multi-school menagerie of buildings at various grade levels called a school district is even more of a challenge. The board would without question be fired if it chose not to hire a superintendent.

Yet, somehow, the same board would permit a superintendent with no expertise in toilets or leaky roofs, or structural issues or electrical or flooring to be the top maintenance person serving as the facility engineer or architect. How can that be? If the superintendent is serving as the maintenance director then there is no Superintendent when the top academic boss available is not wearing his superintendent hat. That is why WBASD is at the bottom of the state's rankings in academic achievement.

The superintendent, brilliant though she or he may be, cannot be an expert in all things. A board in fact that permits dual roles is itself incompetent. How can they permit the extremely high paid young superintendent to perform maintenance decision making and the hiring of contractors and subcontractors and the monitoring of large multi-year projects?

Brian Costello (by title, Superintendent) in his work
as WBASD Architect/Engineer

How many pictures do we need to see of superintendent Brian Costello checking out the Plains work site? By the way, what an ugly site! Is the academic record of the district so high that a superintendent doing superintendent work is not necessary? No, WBASD is ranked 443rd out of 501. How can the superintendent know that construction or repair work is done properly when it is commissioned and finished? Answer. He cannot. That's why buildings enter a state of disrepair far too often when nobody with the proper skillset is taking care of them.

By the way, at 443rd, the Wilkes-Barre Area School District is a lot closer to the bottom of the pack academically than the top. Perhaps the "super" serving as the only architect/engineer on maintenance projects has already taken its toll.

Universities / colleges similar to school districts

When Brian Kelly was employed for 23 years by IBM, one of his roles was to serve as the Higher Education Coordinator working with the ten colleges/universities in Northeastern PA. In this role he was trained to understand how academic institutions were structured and how they operated. He was trained to know what made them tick to help them choose IBM equipment over Brand X.

In his own technical consulting business after he retired from IBM, he had the pleasure of directly supporting Marywood University and College Misericordia and occasionally, he would perform technical consulting work for other Northeastern PA academic institutions such as Luzerne County Community College and King's College.

Kelly tells of the superior maintenance staff Marywood had in place. He viewed them as an outstanding in-house maintenance team. You can still see the results of their fine work all over their beautiful campus. They not only did the normal construction monitoring and facilities job, they also employed craftsmen who remodeled and repurposed facilities for new uses.

For example, this team took the one room Information Technology Department of 1970 and over forty-plus years, Kelly observed them build several new data centers and a new state of the art department with private offices for their analysts, programmers et al. This team was led by a lead Architect/Engineer. When the cost of furniture was high or did not fit the room space, the craftsmen designed and built their own furniture and the result was always first-class and within budget. Besides being part of a great university, he was very impressed with the results of their maintenance team

College Misericordia's facilities maintenance crew were also under the control of an architect when he served as the chief computer technology officer on campus. They had a maintenance plan and were always painting or refurbishing a given area on campus. To save dollars, as the college became a university and expanded their academic programs, they chose to subcontract out their maintenance department while keeping the in-house architect, who reported to the President. The preventive maintenance plan was even more important when the department was outsourced.

Scranton University was not an IBM customer but Brian had a friend, Dave Wilson, who happens to live in South Wilkes-Barre who served as the Architect on the University's many projects. He now serves with the team as a member of the Save Our Schools Group. Scranton U was always building something and everything that they built needed a maintenance plan.

On the University's web site, they tell something about their current team:

"Our Design and Construction department is a service organization responsible for the engineering, planning, documentation, construction, renovation, repair, and maintenance of all University buildings and facilities."

So, why did we just go through the similar methods three different educational institutions use to assure their buildings and facilities are all operational all the time? I have never seen an organization in higher education that did not have an Architect or a maintenance plan. Like the colleges, with $300 million in real-estate assets WBASD cannot function without the expertise of an architect and a well-orchestrated maintenance plan and a staff of building artisans.

The board kids themselves to think they can. When they write their facilities' checks, we will guarantee they are higher than if they had a planned maintenance approach.

Moreover, Kelly cannot recall any buildings ever being ripped down on a local college campus because of their maintenance team's neglect. There are a number of WBASD relics that have been sold and repurposed for business and somehow live-on after the board's Neglect. We see them all across the city. Guthrie is a good example of a building that survived the board.

The Wilkes-Barre Area School Board should have employed these same practices as the small colleges in NEPA and it should employ them in the future regarding maintenance and construction projects. $300 million or more in assets is an awful lot of real property to neglect and ultimately waste.

Whereas WBASB thinks construction planning and control and preventive maintenance are fine when relegated and deferred to the back burner as afterthoughts," organizations that are proper caretakers of their hundreds of millions of dollars' worth of real property assets see facilities management as a vital and even strategic part of their organizations. Without the buildings on campus, how can there be an educational institution? There cannot.

The WBASB and its superintendent have chosen not to use generally accepted facilities management and preventive maintenance procedures. And so, the result is that the long-term health of their facilities has not been assured. That is why at WBASD, buildings like Mackin School in its day, and now Coughlin, GAR & Meyers, are always facing a handy emergency that must be solved or all will be lost.

So, here we are in late 2020, after a number of false starts and blocked decisions about what the board can and should do regarding its ever-changing plans to eliminate Coughlin, GAR, & Meyers—all three City High Schools. This board wants all Wilkes-Barre students to take the bus every day of every school year to their Consolidated Mine Shaft High. What a shame.

And so, since the sane citizens of Wilkes-Barre Area are not suicidal and do not wish to bring on taxpayer bankruptcies by overtaxing themselves or others in the area, many have joined the Save Our Schools Group. This organization is determined to do what is right for the community, regardless of the tyranny, malfeasance, and incompetence of the tyrants serving as members of the board of directors.

The idea of abandoning the notion of neighborhood schools for the one big school fits all idea has never made the taxpayers, parents or students happy or better off wherever it has been implemented—and it is not about to work here. Moreover, from their lousy track record when trusted with major property assets, this board and its young superintendent over the years, put forth clear proof that they cannot handle such big decisions. It is a bungle boondoggle as proposed.

Please consider that they have been serving as the caretakers who permitted all ten of these schools to be neglected and fall into a state of disrepair. Why would anybody with a choice as this consolidated coal-ash toxic-fill monstrosity is forced upon us all, vote to retain this bunch of irresponsible, careless derelicts, whose actions mimic those of imbeciles. Would we not expect that they would take a 40-year school as the Plains school is expected to be, and have it torn down in 25 years. It is their MO.

Just look at the history of the Wilkes-Barre Area School Board and you will believe they are the worst custodians of taxpayer property there could ever be. The secret folks is to vote them out of office as soon as possible. Moreover, anybody who knows an official in the state government, please give them copy of the Big Toxic School 2019 book as well as a copy of both volumes of this book so they can believe it is bad and so that they can stop these renegades in their tracks and turn this folly around for the good of the people. That is what this book is all about. The people do not need a school board full of tyrants who find no problem with figuratively spitting in the public taxpayer's faces. We can definitely do better!

Chapter 13 Final Thoughts on the Three Wilkes-Barre High Schools?

At a recent meeting before Taj Mahal construction began, a member of the community urged the board to keep the three smaller schools as "students learn best in high schools of less than 1000 students." One asks "Why did Shawn Walker a board member who once had similar thoughts, change his mind?" Walker's ideas need to get more traction? Why is the WBA School Board always in such a rush to do the wrong thing?

Never let a good crisis go to waste! The public may not always be willing to pay for good planning but if politicians can create a crisis-- real or perceived, a good-hearted public can be more easily manipulated into rushing into a bad decision. Often power brokers make their decisions and then shape the facts to support their choice-- not necessarily for the good of the public.

Did the School Board decide to rip down the schools before all the analyses even began? I surely don't know the answer, but it appears that there is no will in the WB Press corps to reevaluate this destructive idea. Who are we kidding here? Why does the Board want to build before it even knows what it will build or where it will build it?

How did WB Area come from deciding what to do about the three existing high schools to almost definitely preparing to build a new consolidated high school on Washington St. And, by the way, all of us know that if a new school were to be built, the best locale would have been the Murray Complex. And so this site was summarily eliminated from consideration. Hah!

The reality is that anybody not staring greedily at Tom Wolfe's big pocketbook would conclude that building a new Plasticville model 25-40 year duration school is not the answer. Hey for young officials, in 25 years, they would get to create a new crisis and build a new school again!

In the thick of the turmoil, Kelly spelled out his best plan for the School District. No new consolidated school and it would cost just one to two million dollars per year. Yet, after it was published in the local papers, not one person asked him me about it. Kelly even made "Save our Schools," one of his campaign initiatives in his 2015 losing bid for Mayor of Wilkes-Barre to again bring it to the minds of the public and the school officials. Yet, nobody asked him about it one time during the duration of the campaign. People like leading their own unencumbered lives.

When nobody seeks real input from those with opposing views it typically means the fix is in. This fix will fix it really good for Wilkes-Barre once again. Real good! Does anybody really care? SOS thinks that taxpayers and parents ought to be incensed at what is happening. It is our money and our children's lives that these presbyopic, uncaring leaders are toying with.

One thing we should not do is let Tom Wolfe bully us into making a decision too quickly. We know that haste makes waste; and we are about to waste some wonderful and historically significant school traditions and school buildings—Meyers, GAR and the vacant shell of the Coughlin building—the oldest historical school in PA before it was put to pasture. Moreover, in the process it seems we are willing to sacrifice the opportunity for our children to attend smaller and better run community neighborhood schools and be better educated and be happier than in bully-prone mega schools. Maybe somebody should buy Meyers and make it a charter school?

Think of all of the kids from Larksville, Newport, Swoyersville, Pringle, and Plymouth, who because of the huge Wyoming Valley West jointure years ago never got to play high school sports or who never got to be a big fish in a small pond or get to see how their voice would matter in a setting of their peers. Is this what we really want for Wilkes-Barre Area kids?

By the way. Do we really know what we want? Where is the education plan? What does the new curricula look like? Where is the quality-of-life plan for the school children? Where is the best option plan?

Where there's a will, there is a way. We can surely build anything we want if it is the right thing to do. We must first know what we want.

Don't let them kid you? It starts with dreams, and then ideas, and then plans, and then, and only then does it move to action. Why is nobody dreaming about the ideal situation for Wilkes-Barre Area, the School Children, and the Taxpayers? Does a future with no Coughlin; No GAR; and no Meyers seem like a good idea. Does climbing to the top of Mount Plains sound like an attractive idea for each day after wake-up?

For now, we must decide what our will is in this debacle? A suggestion is that we had better stop this poorly planned project and do some real planning before we take another step in any direction. No immediate decision is always better than a bad decision. Let's not be bullied by the big bad Wolf! If the politicians were not pushing us, what would we want. Taking a bus every day to a Big Toxic School or walking to a neighborhood school close to where we grew up?

Besides the undesirability of the poisonous school on top of a mountain outside of Wilkes-Barre, aren't community neighborhood schools more desirous and more fun than mega cluster consolidated jointures where group think not individual thinking rules every day.

One of your author took a specific position when all this talk began in 2014. Besides suggesting that kids should not have to take the bus to a huge compound school, Brian Kelly's solution to the high-school crisis as written focused on the fact that destroying things is very permanent, especially if it does not further our educational goals.

Special landmarks do not have to be destroyed

The following includes a few snapshots of a letter Kelly wrote to the local papers plus other thoughts. The "I" for a few paragraphs is Mr. Kelly.

The fixes required for WBA School District high schools have been depicted as un-affordable by taxpayers regardless of the approach -- fix it or demolish and build it again cheaper. I don't think so. I don't buy it. It would have been interesting if the numbers and "plans" had been presented at the Wednesday's Board meeting in December 2014 along with the impact on millage. The people remain uninformed even as the Taj Mahal is being built.

We all know the school district has not been a tax bargain for local taxpayers ever. Build or not, the board plans another millage increase this year and next year and next year etc. More importantly for all of us living in Wilkes-Barre Area, the question should be, "Do we really want to destroy historically important well-built school buildings and replace them with cheap quality twenty-five-year models?" Kelly, who is a train aficionado sees this as taking a Plasticville school to replace a marble / granite structure.

Wilkes-Barre High was a marble granite building. The school was established in 1890. It later was renamed Coughlin High after GAR opened in 1925. This old Coughlin school building until decommissioned by our Board, was in fact the oldest public high school building in Pennsylvania.

The shell of the building is still on North Washington St. Can you believe some people want to tear down the oldest public-school building in the State? The Historical Society is not for it folks! The Coughlin Annex structure, next to the marble and granite building was built in 1952.

The original Coughlin building was occupied in 1909 though construction had begun much earlier. Citizens of Wilkes-Barre Area need to get involved and think about what is being proposed and we must ask ourselves if there are not better ways to solve this problem without doubling our already un-affordable school tax burden.

In March, 2005 Cliff Greim may have heard about our plight. Even if not, he wrote an excellent piece titled New Construction vs. Renovation for Older School Facilities. Though ten years old, it still covers the issue quite well. It is available for all to read at http://www.facilitiesnet.com/educationalfacilities/article/School-Choice-Build-New-or-Not--2639#

Greim offers readable counsel on the big decision for WBASD:

"Generally, schools built in the 1950s or earlier have impressive architectural character and often are fixtures in their neighborhoods. They are structurally sound and can accommodate new systems. In addition, there is often strong sentiment to keep them in some form. Still, Wilkes-Barre Area has three such schools in the city of Wilkes-

Barre until the Plains Twp. commissioners offer the School District an occupancy permit a year or so from now. I am praying they won't.

Greim cites in his paper that "Newer schools built in the 1960s and 70s generally lack architectural character, are not energy-efficient and are constructed of cheaper materials. These get torn down more often or become hand-me-down conversions from high schools to junior highs or from junior highs to elementary schools." Plasticville train schools made by Lionel may have more useful life than the consolidated Big Toxic School.

All of the buildings in question (Coughlin, GAR, and Meyers were built post 1950 other than the Coughlin Annex, which was built in 1952. I think it is safe to say that the same logic Greim discusses for pre-1950 buildings apply to the Coughlin Annex.

I admit I was taken back by board members at last night's meeting who said, "It's going to cost a lot but it's something we have to do." I would ask whether they would vote to tear down historic Independence Hall if it were within their responsibility back in 1860 when it was just over 100 years old. It helps to know that at that time, this famous Philadelphia structure was about the same age as Coughlin was about the time of its retirement?

We all know that Independence Hall is the birthplace of America. We also know that the Declaration of Independence and the U.S. Constitution were both debated and signed inside this remarkable building. Independence Hall was built between 1732 and 1756 to be the Pennsylvania State House. It still stands and thrives. Why can Philadelphia preserve a monument and Wilkes-Barre cannot?

Originally, this building housed all three branches of Pennsylvania's colonial government. Yes, it was built even before the USA became the USA. It is now two and a half times older than Coughlin High School and it has a lot of life left. Hopefully, you have been there and you also got a glimpse of the one and only Liberty Bell. Hopefully the WBASB would not rip down a famous WBA school bell if one could be found?

Think of the famous graduates of Coughlin, GAR, and Meyers, and think of all the memorable events at those schools. These buildings are special landmarks in our home area, and they do not have to be destroyed.

GAR is almost ninety years old and Meyers is the baby at just more than 85 years of age. Why would we give up these historically significant well-built structures and replace them with thirty-year throwaway square buildings made of sheet metal, plastic, and other cheap materials? We have historical buildings with grand designs, granite and limestone interiors, and exquisite stained-glass auditoriums.

Who are we to cast this all away so that in twenty years another study like this can be done as we rip out the structures to be built and go with even cheaper buildings with twenty-year lifetimes or perhaps a modular school or a few trailers? Where there is a will, there is a way. Somehow Wilkes-Barre residents lost our will with the Sterling Hotel's elimination after spending $6 million without fixing the roof. Let's keep our will and our wits this time as the board tries to shove a huge millage increase our way... for a less desirable outcome than the status quo.

One off-hand suggestion I have is to allocate about a million dollars or two or perhaps three if we can afford it while saving $121 million in construction costs. We can bring in a great building contractor from our area to allocate five or ten artisans just for WBA, to begin work on these buildings, one year at a time, one objective at a time.

Let's get the hazards out of the way first. When real emergencies occur in the other buildings, we can dispatch this crew of experts along with WBA maintenance personnel to fix the problems post haste. All immediate maintenance would be done immediately while a plan for maintaining all the District's buildings can be built concurrently.

I would also use our political representatives to get waivers for the beams that can withstand lateral forces. This is a very costly undertaking and should be ruled out immediately.

Clearly all of the WBA buildings in question have not been blown over by big puffs of wind in the 85 to 105 years in which they have been standing and they are not going to be blown over tomorrow or any time soon.

I would also try to get waivers for increasing the physical size of the classrooms. They seem big enough to have been able to be used for conducting classes for many years and surely they could continue to be used. Waivers would save a lot of money and they are practical and safe.

I would bet that the local and state historical societies would help in gaining the waivers. How can we consider destroying such history in three marble and granite forever buildings that have lasted at least 85 years, for a promise we know will be broken thirty years from now. After all, citizens make the laws. If the laws do not fit, waivers are a good way to save money and still have the benefits of a safe school.

When all the emergencies are fixed, I would put the new team of artisans to work on one floor at a time of one building at a time. I would use as many vocational students to help in the effort as possible. Think of the training they would get. Additionally, Wilkes-Barre Area also has a lot of maintenance / custodial personnel, who I bet would love to learn new skills working with the best artisans in the valley in building, plumbing, electrical, carpentry and other endeavors. Where there is a will, there is a way. Nothing in life truly worth having is easy. Why give up the best for a solution that may not even be good enough to be called "second-best?"

Chapter 14 Do You Trust the WBA School Board?

Can you count on the board that brought us the contaminated mine waste site for The Big Toxic School to do the right thing for the people?

It all adds up to an absurd problem for Wilkes-Barre Area. Every book must have a plot. The plot for this book is to identify the serious problems that have been part of the history of the Wilkes-Barre Area School District as managed by what an honest evaluation would say is an incompetent, or inept, or a corrupt school board. This book is needed so that the identified problems can be solved in the most appropriate manner. Perhaps it is really the following questions which must be answered to forge ahead: "Is this the best way to govern public schools."

As noted in Chapter 2, the purpose of this book is motivated by a tyrannical board. Hope is given to the public that a resolution can be found by reviewing three movies. In each of the three movies, after being wronged, the people were vindicated and made whole. The first movie, "Bad Education," stars Hugh Jackman

https://en.wikipedia.org/wiki/Bad_Education_(2019_film).

It is the true story of the Roslyn School District on Long Island New York where millions of tax dollars were stolen. The movie has been well received. Though it makes one think a bit of Wilkes-Barre Aera in its highlighting of board and top official corruption, The WBA tale has so many facets, it makes "Bad Education" look like a Disney cartoon.

Luzerne County, the home of the Wilkes-Barre School District is infamous for another true movie titled "Kids for Cash." In this story, two judges took kickbacks for every juvenile that they incarcerated in private detention centers.

Their objective was to increase occupancy at the for-profit detention centers in which they were highly invested. The judges were known for disposing of thousands of children for extended stays in youth centers for offenses as trivial as mocking an assistant principal on Myspace or trespassing in a vacant building. Until mid-2020, both judges were in the Big House. They may be there for some time to come.

The third motivator to fight the Wilkes-Barre Area School Board (WBASB) is another movie from March 2000. This movie is titled Erin Brockovich. It is a true story starring the famous Hollywood actress Julia Roberts.

Brockovich fought against the energy corporation Pacific Gas and Electric Company (PG&E). When she began digging into the case, she found evidence that the groundwater in the town of Hinkley had been seriously contaminated with carcinogenic hexavalent chromium. This happens to be the same type of carcinogen found in the building site for the WBA Big Toxic High School. However, she also discovered that PG&E had been telling the public lies that their water contained a safer form of chromium. Eventually, Brockovich and the town won the case. Has the WBASB been telling the public the truth?

In all three cases, the public won the cases and so the Save Our Schools (SOS) group is continually encouraged by these movies to tell the story of the long-time corrupt Wilkes-Barre School Board. Obviously, this active group (SOS) is seeking a resolution for the School Board's malfeasance and misfeasance and nonfeasance and is working to make its record four for four on selected movies.

Now, let's talk some more about this toxic, poisonous story. It helps to remember as we recount this that Wilkes-Barre Area School Board did not have to build a school on a toxic mine site. It was a problem which they could have easily avoided. In fact, they had to go through great pains in order to make their ruse all seem legitimate.

Nonetheless, with many better choices to be had, the board chose the Big Toxic School Site. Just one of those reasons was to spite Wilkes-Barre PA for not granting them a permit on their first opportunity to make money on the deal.

In the Brockovich story summary above, you recall that PG&E told the residents of Hinkley that the hexavalent chromium was at a very light level. It is exactly what SOS and Wilkes-Barre Area has been told by the legal folks from the WBASB.

In March 2020, as testing continued during construction, Michael Krzywicki of Apollo Group Inc., the district's building project manager, gave a report on the project at a Monday Board meeting. He was quick to say that lab results showed no detectable amount of hexavalent chromium, a carcinogen often found in coal ash. "No Detectable" Hmmmm! Who pays Krzywicki? Hmmmm!! Follow the money!

Most of the arsenic levels from the latest testing were below the non-resident direct contact limit of 61 mg/kg, and most arsenic levels were between 15-25 mg/kg, Krzywicki said. "Most?"

The highest reading was 50.6 mg/kg around a detention basin along Maffett Street. The state Department of Environmental Protection is requiring an additional 6 inches of topsoil there and the placement of a visual barrier in the soil to indicate if soil erosion actually takes place, Krzywicki said.

If it sounds a lot like he said; she said, without a jury. It is! There is no maintenance, architectural, or engineering expertise working for the School District to protect us. Are all contractors on the take? So, how would they know?

Dear Reader, ask yourself if Roslyn is as nasty a story as WBASB. Why would this corrupt board—and we say corrupt because there is no other plausible way to look at it—why did they all go against all sound reasoning to forge ahead with their dastardly plan to make kids sick in Plains Township despite hearing many, many objections.

The board chose a building site for a new high school that is a former coal mining site used as a coal ash dump and industrial waste dump—a double whammy! The site is subsidence prone, with levels of arsenic cancer-causing chemicals. In the last election, hoping to eliminate the board that did this, international non-fiction writer Brian W. Kelly published a book, called "The Big Toxic School." In this book, Kelly brought to the forefront this sordid "Tale of Corruption, Deception, Taxation, & Tyranny." The citizens almost unseated the Board. Almost in our case is not close enough.

The Wilkes-Barre School Board has been accustomed for many years to having its way. When nepotism did not work, cronyism was used. When cronyism failed, they used favoritism. The public saw so much corruption over the years from this board and its fore boards, that there had to be some great board payoffs that were kept a secret until enough board members did their individual time in the Big House.

To be specific over time, the school district had four board members indicted by the FBI and jailed for fraud. The corruption was so prevalent that three of the members were WBASB board presidents at the time of their removals. Some think they pocketed the most based on their titles. The most recent past board president faced a life sentence for extortion, having forged the signatures of judges to gain favors for incarcerated inmates in the Luzerne County prison. He carried an illegal weapon, and he used and distributed drugs to the inmates.

Then there are other long-term board members who had their problems, though less than being sentenced to jail, they were noteworthy none the less. One member, who was not indicted, was embarrassed by a DUI, though seemingly not too embarrassed. He was a regular on Facebook etc. posting on social media joking about another teacher having oral sex with a student. Funny right? He is still on the board after retiring from a career as a WBA administrator. WBASD just can't get rid of these guys.

The other 8 board members are not as open about their issues because all eight of them at the time, as well as the hired superintendent asked for this board member's resignation, but he refused to step down. For their own reasons, they decided not to force the issue. You can get away with anything by being on this board. Instead, he stayed on the board and is still on the board.

The book that was written about the board's action titled The Big Toxic School is well known across the country for its subtitle: Wilkes-Barre Area's Tale of Corruption, Deception, Taxation & Tyranny. Pick the non-compliment from the sub-title that best fits the recalcitrant board member and it describes the public perception of them all pretty well. They are not very respected.

The Wilkes-Barre School Board made lots of mistakes and continues to make them because no higher authority has yet to remove their authority. The chain of costly errors and omissions, nepotism, cronyism, potential fraud, coupled with building a high school on an unlined coal ash dump rivals the travails of the Erin Brockovich tale.

Can it be Absurd?

Some suggest that absurdity is the quality or state of being ridiculous or wildly unreasonable. The Wilkes-Barre Area School Board has been behaving in an absurd manner for many years, especially in recent years. Sometimes they go to jail. Sometimes they just pull bone head acts and stay in their positions to show the people who is really the boss.

Building on a toxic site to spite a major city is clearly absurd. Nonetheless, the state environmental authority, DEP, who also may suffer a bit of nepotism, cronyism, and favoritism, has given approval to build a school on a poisonous site and it then must apparently monitor and assure the safety of the new high school project. Sure! The truth, however, is that before they audited, they already know that the toxic ingredients that compose this site make it impossible to build and for it to be safe. Yet the trotted onward in approval.

An intensive and honest site evaluation by the PA DEP was supposedly completed and an additional third-party review was done by Tetra Tech. The site engineers, the district construction manager, the high-paid solicitor, the top pay receiving superintendent and the work-for free board have consistently answered reporters and citizens questions posed at board meetings regarding concerns about the site.

The reports are not a secret. All are available on the district website. Regardless of all the rhetoric, citizens do not feel too good about their kids breathing toxic air and parents do not feel good about paying the huge hundred plus-million-dollar tab. It is all part of the toxic site scenario on the contaminated mine waste site. Was the entire City of

Wilkes-Barre and surrounds duped by a neighborhood board with an agenda and "big wheel connections?"

Board members have a tough time explaining to voters how this school will save money in the long run. Each election brings in less of the culpable board as they are partially reelected as the community wakes up to the deceit. There is always something missing with this board. For example, reports show there was supposedly a reduction of approximately $3.5 million in operating costs that was supposed to offset the cost of construction. Nobody can verify if this was smoke or reality. Has it really happened? Will it really happen?

Many regular people living in the community understandably fear taxes will climb constantly to pay for this monstrous expensive Taj-Mahal-like school consolidation. For example, right now, among other things, the local papers reported that the Wilkes-Barre Area School District is 33 million dollars underfunded by the state. This is according to the State's Basic Education Formula. How does the board make up this difference? Do they even care?

Taxes have climbed because of state mandated expenditures such as Charter Schools, Special Education and pensions that continually increase. The board says the selection of a consolidated school is a cost control method that will allow the district to save money. Nobody can refute the all-omnipotent board.

Most residents are not buying that. There is no proof because there has been no investigation and though the Board expounds that it will keep taxes under control, SOS projects that taxes will grow out of control to as high as a half-billion dollars. The people do not believe the board. The juristocracy is for the officials and against the plebeians.

It is absurd that the school district is underfunded by $33 million from the state and nobody is complaining at a healing level. At the same time, with a lack of funding, the area's population is at a poverty level. Wilkes-Barre Area treasures every new dollar it finds, and it finds very few. The average wage is the lowest in the state. Yet, this board is ready to sock it to the poor people of the Wilkes-Barre Area for its own gains.

So, for the school consolidation's supposed savings, the Board thinks the solution is to close the three existing high schools in the major tax base in the area—Wilkes-Barre City. Theoretically this is to save the taxpayer's money. People in the know understand that consolidation is an outdated costly means of saving money and it isn't going to happen even with this project plan.

Meanwhile the people of Wilkes-Barre who seem to have no choice but to enroll in the Big Toxic School, more and more are plotting to form a charter school in Wilkes-Barre City, perhaps in one of the old city High Schools such as Meyers. The health of WB City students would be enhanced by not having to breather in the toxic air on this polluted mountain.

Using inflated renovation costs and ignoring a potential forever shelf life on renovated, old well-built granite and marble buildings, the board selected the district owned Coughlin site. Despite historic significance, the Board expressed a deep desire to demolish this historic school. At the same time, it chose in iteration 1, to build a new consolidated school by South Washington Street tracks, but Wilkes-Barre City would not permit it with its long-standing zoning laws.

It was absurd that the board squandered $6 million on an idea with no permit authorizing the expenditure. The zoning request failed but first the district spent $6 million. Who got the $6 million? It clearly was not the citizens.

Bad Education would have found the cash lining, not having originally been willing to wait for the zoning decision. The WBASB board impatiently felt that it faced aging facilities that needed a lot of immediate work and publicly expressed their belief that trying to expand Coughlin was the expeditious way to a solution. Moreover, they appeared to believe that their absurd plan would have no problem being approved by the City. The best laid plans of mice and men aft gang agley.

However, the downtown site which preceded the selection of the Big Toxic School site was as the pundits would say, absurd. It was actually asinine. The super and the board officials knew the site did not meet the minimum space requirement required by the state for a high school (which the WBASB officials and legal staff should have known).

Six million dollars was put in Michael Jackson's Netherland and thus the Board wasted funds put forth by a trusting impoverished school district. It was not a caring set of board members for sure or they would not have blown the taxpayers money on nothing at all—not something to gain them benefit.

What absurd notion duped them? Despite the almost certainty of failure without a permit, the board agreed to lease a 90-year-old building for 20 years. Absurd! Yes!

In this scheme, the board's team also decided to destroy another City school, a monument to great building projects in the 1920's and 1930's —Meyers High School bragging that the soil conditions were not right on the site with the big stadium and noting that it would have no option but to demolish the school and the entire site. What kind of soils conditions?

Ironically, all the years before this declaration and all the years after, the Board kept Meyers in its stable of schools without a peep of this doomsday ultimate potentiality. What prompted the destroy and rebuild mentality? When they needed Meyers to last, they became quiet as church mice about the irreparable soil condition.

Moreover, this was also despite a building already on the Meyers site--Kistler Elementary across Meyers stadium in Miner Park. It had already been deemed ok enough to add a WBASB board-approved building addition of $27 million to the same building – an elementary school. How can this be. It is absurd. It's the only excuse. Is absurdity corruption or is it incompetence or ineptness or is it all three?

One of your authors, Brian Kelly tells his story about marrying a GAR Girl. Being a Meyers guy, she had to be pretty. She is still very pretty fifty years later. I know that Grenadiers love their school no matter how old they get. GAR High School was put back into its best shape in many years after its recent remodeling. When the Board chose to save Meyers and grow Coughlin, they originally found no place for GAR and did not even consider GAR in their considerations.

So, they began to think of configurations with middle schools. Since they had no place preordained in their big plans for GAR High School, even though middle schools as a district configuration strategy had previously been ruled out by the same Board. GAR now seemed to fit the bill. That my friends is absurd and it is the product of no planning.

The best part of this seriously flawed, potentially illegal plan was the renovation, not the expansion of, a previously shuttered elementary school--Mackin School sized for 500 students. For its own reasons, the Board had completely remodeled Mackin even though it had not been in use for years. Perhaps one of their construction buddies needed a job. Who knows for sure. Nobody trusts the board's building decisions. In fact, few trust that any of the board's decisions will benefit the people of WBA.

Not thinking straight again, the board decided to place 800 high school students from a prematurely closed Coughlin High School into the formerly shuttered Mackin school temporarily until the Board got its musical buildings straightened out.

The cost was considered insignificant at $9 million. The board knew it was just poor people paying for the renovations so nobody of consequence would complain. The not-approved Coughlin consolidation was to replace the former Coughlin and Meyers. Then, CHS closed "unexpectedly." Though many thought they would be going to Meyers, which had the room, the CHS students were not moved to Meyers. Instead, they were moved to the formerly shuttered Mackin Elementary. The board made off like it was part of the plan all-along and that much considered went towards this move. But, in retrospect, it too is absurd.
It was physically possible with a few moderations costing a tremendous lot less than $9 million that another option including Meyers in the mix could have been effected. GAR had not been explicitly highlighted for change. This plan had to incorporate the segregation of 800 GAR students, as a substantial proportion of the school population were minorities. GAR had never been considered in the "beneficial" consolidation, but they did have the highest percentage of minorities.

This board action led to a news story stating that racism is alive and well, by the executive director of NAACP. Is this information absurd enough? Because it is still not the worst.

When the City refused to give the board a zoning permit to build in Wilkes-Barre City, the board decided to punish Wilkes-Barre City for not doing the board's wishes. With a young like a kid, boy-faced superintendent, labeled as such by one of the local papers, the board should have expected childish antics from the new boss because they got them in spades.

When rebuffed by the City of Wilkes-Barre's Zoning Dept., the board literally packed up its flip charts and power points from South Washington Street and they went looking for another place. To find a place for their world class ignominy, this board is ready to shut down the Empire State Building if it had to, to get its will done. The three Wilkes-Barre schools had no chance of surviving in Wilkes-Barre proper and they still don't unless this two-book set works.

Meanwhile the WBA board unleashed its venom on the City while looking anywhere else but Wilkes-Barre for a new site. One looking at the spiteful reaction of the baby-faced superintendent for not getting his way, one might conclude that if he had to build a school in Goose Island that would be OK with him—as long as it were not in Wilkes-Barre.

But, he might be convicted of murder for that so the plan of building a new consolidated toxic school outside of Wilkes-Barre City looked like it would serve the Superintendent and the board in such a way as to permit them to live after the project was completed.
This very young and not necessarily very wise board superintendent was over-heard after a recent board meeting saying "Now, it's any place for the new school but Wilkes-Barre." Wilkes-Barre City had to be taught by the WBASB that it is not nice to fool with a young, inexperienced, vindictive, superintendent. Can anything be more absurd?

What if I told you that only 7 sites were considered out of 124 square miles of pristine land? Only three non-district sites, two of which were coal mining family owned, Biscontini and Pagnotti, were part of the mix of possibilities. We have not examined if the family coal barons had any connections with the decisions made to favor them. But, surely it is possible.

Of interest besides Plains was a Wilkes-Barre City site called the Murray Complex in downtown Wilkes-Barre. It is just a mile from Holy Redeemer High School. And, so it had already been zoned OK for high schools. But the intemperate Superintendent had nixed Wilkes-Barre and was looking out of the boundaries of the major district municipality. The superintendent and his wife earn their hefty salary through WBASD but live in Mountain Top so their taxes go to Crestwood School district along with their children.

Despite it having passed its own zoning test for school construction not too, too long ago, when Holy Redeemer HS was built, the board decided not to test this great site with another zoning hearing and the risk of raising the kid superintendent's ire. Instead, the primary game plan was that Wilkes-Barre City had to be punished. This Murray Complex therefore was rejected by the wise men on the board and the young superintendent, supposedly for the safety of the children.

They said that it was adjacent to a busy city street and near railroad tracks. This was a bogus reason as the same street bordered Holy Redeemer High. City residents knew from widespread hearsay that the Board pulled out of Wilkes-Barre to punish the City for not permitting the school to be built by not granting the building permit.

So, in the final analysis, the board's chosen safest best site was the worst that could be found anyplace in the country. Perhaps the Three Mile Island in PA might be a worst site—maybe. But just perhaps. And it is not in the U.S. Just like the Catholic High School, it would be adjacent to everything bad—the superhighway Cross-Valley expressway, near railroad tracks, a strip and deep mined coal ash dump, with cancer causing arsenic, and prone to subsidence.

After wasting six million dollars on the no-go at Coughlin consolidation, the board was seemingly desperate to find a quick deal. They agreed to pay five times the lowest assessed value for a former industrial waste dump site. Do they require competency tests for board members and superintendents in Pennsylvania?

The Board tried to justify it by a $3.2 million-dollar bogus and corrupt mineral rights purchase to show its legitimacy was never appraised. Did somebody on the know or one of the owners make a killing on this undocumented transaction? If we asked to show us the money? What would we find? Why else would they make such an obviously poor decision. The board action authorized the purchase at or higher than the property's assessed value. How did they justify that?

The board purchased the property for $4.2 million with appraisals in hand from $250,000 to a high of $800,000. Is this paragraph absurd enough? It continues. The board spent millions when it did not have to do so. Why? Who profited? One would think that all efforts for a school board that produces poor academic achievement as its main product would make all its decisions to better student outcomes. Not this School Board? Why not? What motivated this board to go against the wishes of a community to serve its own ends? Was there a pot at the end of the rainbow? There sure are a lot of great salaries and stipends even if no pot.

Maybe they did not care what their principal job as board members actually was. Everybody knows that the academic achievement results from this board's leadership is lots closer to last in the state than first. No expenditure that does nothing for academic achievement should ever have been made in the Wilkes-Barre Area.

The Big Toxic School is undoubtably the least prudent of all the Board's decisions in which students have been involved.
To repeat, the #1 problem in the WBASD is student achievement. It is nonexistent. It ranks near the bottom of all school districts statewide. National education research and the opinions and results of neighboring districts show that consolidation would definitely make it worse. So, did the School Board decide to consolidate even though they knew it would not be good for the students or the taxpayers. They sure did!

National educational research and our own studies state that closing the neighborhood schools is a major disadvantage academically. Neighborhood schools enhance the education process. Despite the evidence, the WBASB decided to close all three neighborhood high schools in Wilkes-Barre City, the major community in the district.

Research and our own studies list middle schools as a disadvantage. So the board decided as an intermediate decision to have two middle schools. Experts know that community (neighborhood) schools link students, families, and communities to educate children and strengthen neighborhoods. They have become a popular model for education in many US cities in part because they build on community assets and address multiple determinants of educational disadvantage. Big schools, especially big toxic consolidated schools are outmoded and do not produce such positive outcomes. Since community schools seek to have an impact on populations, not just the children enrolled, they provide an opportunity to improve community health.

Stripping the largest community in a school district of all of its community schools decreases that community's chance at achieving excellent academic results, though sports results may fare better. Community schools influence the health and education of neighborhood residents through three pathways: building trust, establishing norms, and linking people to networks and services.

Through such services as school-based health centers, nutrition education, family mental health counseling, violence prevention, and sexuality education, these schools build on the multiple reciprocal relationships between health and education. By developing closer ties between community schools and neighborhood health programs, public health professionals can help to mobilize a powerful new resource for reducing the health and educational inequalities that now characterize US cities. We suggest an agenda for research, practice, and policy that can build the evidence needed to guide such a strategy. Risking student health by forcing students to attend large schools built on toxic mine chemical disposal sites clearly does not assist in maintaining positive health results.

Problem # 2, underfunded $33 million a year in a poverty level district. We enter a potential half BILLION-dollar project with no long-range curriculum/facility master plan for only 2400 hundred students leaving 4500 in the balance, for three facilities to one leaving 6 other aged facilities out: estimated renovation costs $67 million.

Problem #3 Facilities. Covered in paragraph one.

Problem # 4. Due to the dire straits of student achievement, financial woes, and facilities, required qualified, credible experience at the district and board levels, including contracted professional services. A solicitor who said zoning can't fail; kids need to eat coal ash to be harmed; the deeds convey mineral rights, they didn't; the site is worth $4.2 million based on un-assessed mineral rights.

Three (restorable) historic schools in the balance, not one but four architect firms hired with zero large school restoration experience, and sparse large school construction experience. Plus, no in-house engineering or architectural expertise and no plans to hire a competent maintenance crew or develop a maintenance plan even for the new building.

Provided with the opportunity to hire the two top district positions, the board hires a superintendent and business manager that never held the positions prior. At the board level, at a time when experience was mandated, a former district clerk is made board president, over four master's degree holders.

Credibility? Four former board members jailed for pay to play activities. A board president faced a life sentence for among a large list of chargers, extortion. Need we add substance abuse, moral issues, and racism, board role models? Has this document met, if not exceeded the definition of absurd?
Held in high esteem (years back) were community volunteers (unpaid) that carried the revered title, Board of Education Director— only exceeded by Board President. Major corporations and banks encouraged their employees to run for school boards. Five years back community leaders, Save Our Schools Inc. attempted to recruit people to run for the school board; not successful. Although we did get a retired grandmother to run and she is on the board. Adding two more this last election.

SOS attempted to get a bank executive to run in the past election, he was told the bank was concerned. Two realtors were interested but felt it would be negative on their business. The exact opposite to, back in 1968 when WBASD was nationally acclaimed for academic achievements.

Why the reluctance to serve? Four board members conducting a pay to play scheme with district positions from custodians, teachers, administrators, and venders, went to jail. An FBI indicted board member a month later was elected board president. A second board president, bring the total to five WBA board members, faced a life sentence for among many charges, extortion and forged signatures of sitting judges. A recent board member while the board was in session gawked at his cell phone which had a half-naked woman on the screen.

The W-B police frequented his home for alleged drug distribution and potential brothel activity. A sitting board member (retired WBA administrator) arrested for a DUI, was labeled by police and hospital security as belligerent, and felt that as a board member he should not have been arrested. Same board member, frequent social media poster posted that an AZ teacher having oral sex with a student as humorous and posted concern that she might have broken teeth.

Another post a picture of ethnic link sausage which he disgustingly described as turds. Another post bordered on homophobic, posting the word "fag." Latest was his opinion on not allowing the confederate flag. One hundred and ninety-two replies, including a fellow board member stating as a board member he should not have taking such a stand publicly. For the first time in the hundred-year history of the board, eight members and the superintendent requested his resignation. They did not get it. That too is absurd.

Then we have a retired WBA attendance clerk, an executive on the board, on whose computer put out over 10 raciest e-mails that put disadvantaged students down. Her reply was that someone used her computer when she was on coffee breaks. Her social media posts clearly indicate missing filters, I don't give a crap, or supporting a posting that put down Mexicans and Methodists. There was another very insensitive posting, a reply to a citizen providing her reasonable input. Theses postings and others put validity to the possibility that she did the racist and derogatory e-mails

The situation in Wilkes-Barre Area School District not only seems absurd when you read about it, it is even more absurd when you live through it and watch this Board in action.

Chapter 15 Can You Get My Nephew or Wife a Job?

Addressing and Correcting WBASD Hiring Problems

The highest position that the Wilkes-Barre Area School Board brought-on as an employee in recent times is titled Superintendent of Schools. This is such a major position; it would be appropriate for the board to conduct what it called a nationwide formal search to assure the best person for the job is found and hired. This idea spawns the question: "Did the board conduct a formal search?" for such an important position?

There was some effort expended in the process which gave the board a level of credence in the hiring even though it may have not been done according to Hoyle. A review shows that it was not much more that a half-baked attempt to cover the lack of an earnest search. With this as a backdrop, we must ask the following question for discussion:

Should paying $11,000 to the Pa. School Boards Association, an organization that is not an official search agency, to conduct the search be properly categorized as a "formal search?" Other than the board, most officials would answer that question in the negative.

Here is what we found. Seventeen real applicants applied, but just a dozen or so had real experience in that they actually served as superintendents. Brian Costello, the boy-faced official who got the job without much competition, was not one of the dozen. Brian had no years as an assistant superintendent or as a superintendent. He did have a total of 4 years as an assistant principal, and he pit 4 years in at the central office as director of curriculum responsible for "student achievement."

Considering that Costello was in charge of student achievement when it began to slip. So was the mere fact that he held the position enough to warrant hiring him? In other words, how did that work out? WBASD is now ranked #443 / 501 in the state of PA. Seems like the academic achievement in the Costello years is not as good as one might expect for a Board paying top dollar for its Superintendent. Researching this issue, we were told by a board member that they

had one especially good applicant but that they could not afford what that person wanted in salary. Looking at the District's academic achievement recently an observe might suggest that perhaps the bigger truth is that the board could not afford not to hire such a qualified applicant.

What would you think is the primary cause of poor results in an organization such as a school district or a business enterprise? For example, poor results for our school district would be as it is – one of the lowest ranks in academic achievement in the state. The wise answer is poor management. Poor management is the cause of many failures in businesses and institutions. If the students aren't learning what we teach maybe we such teach the way students learn. New management with a positive track record often brings in better methods by which to achieve much better results.

Bad management can impact employees and an organization's overall operations. Incompetent managers are often hired but they can also grow in place. They can have challenges relating to staff members such as keeping staff motivated. In addition, substandard supervisors may not be able to balance budgets, increase revenues or capably perform other crucial tasks. A tid-bit for the WBASB is that if district employees complain about working for your management team, investigate the claims so your organization doesn't suffer irreparably from poor leadership.

Like most organizations or businesses that fail in their main role, the problems with the Wilkes-Barre Area School District all spawn from bad management. No greater sign that the problems are malignant and unsolvable is when an organization has an opportunity to change its leadership and better itself and instead, it chooses patronage or favoritism in hiring. Resorting to nepotism or cronyism makes big management problems eternally unsolvable. Think about it.

Patronage is defined as the control of or power to make appointments to government jobs or the power to grant other political favors. Favoritism, cronyism, and nepotism are ways in which patronage is often distributed. Patronage itself has several meanings but in the hiring of personnel it has a simple definition. Patronage is the control of or power to make appointments to government jobs or the power to grant other political favors.

When Bernard Prevuznak announced for example, in February, 2016, that the Wilkes-Barre Area School Board had a plum position to offer the "right" person—the top position in the District—was it competence or nepotism or patronage that caused Brian James Costello to gain that position. How did it happen? Was he the best guy in the country for the job? Has he performed as well as the top billing he received?

As favoritism is the broadest of these related terms, we'll start with its definition. Basically favoritism is just what it sounds like; it's favoring a person not because he or she is doing the best job but rather because of some extraneous feature such as membership in a favored group, personal likes and dislikes, being the nephew of somebody important, etc. Favoritism can be demonstrated in hiring, wage increases, as well as honoring, or awarding contracts.

A related idea to favoritism is patronage, giving public service jobs to those who may have helped elect the person who has the power of appointment. Often those who are hired from patronage practice patronage Favoritism has always been a major complaint in government service.

In 2002, a survey from the federal government's Office of Personnel Management found that only 36.1 percent of federal workers thought promotions in their work units were based on merit. (Government Executive Magazine, "Playing Favorites," by Brian Friel, October 2004). They believed that connections, partisanship, and other factors played a more important role.

Cronyism is a more specific form of favoritism, referring to partiality towards friends and associates. As the old saying goes, "It's not what you know but who you know," or, as blogger Danny Ferguson put it, "It's not what you don't know; it's who your college roommate knows." Cronyism occurs within a network of insiders-of the "good ol' boys," who confer favors on one another.

Nepotism is an even narrower form of favoritism. Coming from the Italian word for nephew, it covers favoritism to members of the family. Both nepotism and cronyism are often at work when political parties recruit candidates for public office. A job is something the recipient often feels they owe lifetime allegiance to the benefactor. So giving a job has benefits sometime exceeding those of receiving a job. Thee better the job the bigger the benefits may be.

What do favoritism, cronyism, and nepotism have to do with ethics? One of the most basic themes in ethics is fairness, stated this way by Artistotle: "Equals should be treated equally and unequals, unequally." Favoritism, cronyism, and nepotism all interfere with fairness because they give undue advantage to someone who does not necessarily merit this treatment. In the public sphere, favoritism, cronyism, and nepotism also undermine the common good. When someone is granted a position because of connections rather than because he or she has the best credentials and experience for the job, the service that person renders to the public often is inferior.

Also, because favoritism is often covert (few elected officials are foolish enough to show open partiality to friends, and family), this practice undercuts the transparency that should be part of governmental hiring and contracting processes.

What ethical dilemmas do favoritism, cronyism, and nepotism present? Probably the biggest dilemma presented by favoritism is that, under various other names, few people see it as a problem. Connections, networking, family—almost everyone has drawn on these sources of support in job hunting in the private sphere. Substitute favoritism and the picture becomes clearer. And everyone can point to instances where cronyism or nepotism is an accepted fact of life in a political sphere, as well.

John F. Kennedy, for example, appointed his brother Robert as Attorney General. Every president and governor names close associates to key cabinet positions. Mayors put those they know and trust on citizens committees and commissions. Friends and family can usually be counted on for loyalty, and officeholders are in a good position to know their strengths.

So, what's the problem? The first issue is competence. Without the pressure of favoritism, nepotism, or cronyism, for cabinet level positions, an executive will more than likely be drawn to experienced, qualified candidates, but historically, the lower down the ladder, the more likely it is for someone's brother-in-law or nephew to be slipped into a job for which he is not qualified.

The American Civil Service Act was passed in 1883 in large part because so many patronage jobs, down to dogcatcher, were being filled by people whose only qualification for employment was their support for a particular party or candidate. Also, the appearance of favoritism weakens morale in government service, not to mention public faith in the integrity of government. Everybody has been victimized in their career by favoritism so we all know this is true.

Reasonable people will differ about the appointment of friends and family in high-level positions, but public officials should be aware that such choices can give the appearance of unfairness. According to the National Conference of State Legislatures, 19 state legislatures have found the practice of nepotism troubling enough to enact laws against it. Others may restrict the hiring of relatives or friends in more general conflict-of-interest rules.

Public officials should also note that dilemmas involving favoritism extend beyond hiring and contracting practices to the more general problem of influence and more sleazy notion of influence peddling. Golfing partners, people who come over for Sunday dinner, members of the same congregation etc.—all are likely to exert a greater influence over an official than a stranger might. Think about it.

Council members, mayors, and legislators must make special efforts to ensure that they hear all sides of an issue rather than just relying on the views of the people they know. Further, many conscientious lawmakers have discovered that they must change their patterns of socializing when their work involves many decisions affecting friends and associates. At the least, they may choose to recuse themselves from votes where social relationships may exert undue influence.

The Role of the School Board and the Superintendent

Most of us know that a school board consists of lay representatives – people who live in the community and are selected (elected) by the community. In some other communities, the school board can be appointed, or the school board is selected by either the mayor or county freeholders.

In essence, the members are your neighbors: parents, grandparents, local business owners, retirees—ordinary citizens. They are supposed to be non-partisan and they receive no pay or benefits for their public service. Since they come from the same community, technically, they share the same interests and concerns about the school district as do other residents of the community.

So, what is the role of the school board and the superintendent? The school board has a dual role: To represent the concerns of the citizens, taxpayers and parents to the school administrators, and to represent the needs of the students and school district to the citizens, taxpayers and parents of the community. The school board does not operate the district on a day-to-day basis; that is the job of the superintendent, who is the district's chief executive. Rather, the school board sets the policies, goals and objectives for the district – and it holds the superintendent responsible for implementing the policies and achieving the goals.

The superintendent is hired by the school board. While the board's focus is governance and oversight of management, the superintendent's focus is on implementation and management. The superintendent in many ways is the Chief Executive Officer of the School District—the top banana so to speak. It is also most often the position which commands the highest salary.

How does a superintendent get chosen by the board?

The Reading Eagle (Pennsylvania) says that there is way too much nepotism and cronyism in their school District. The same can be said of the Wilkes-Barre Area School District. Some go so far as to say that in WBASD, the current superintendent is the product of nepotism post facto. Did the WBASB conduct a formal search for its superintendent? We discussed this in the beginning of the chapter. In retrospect, looking at the district's state rankings in academic achievement as noted, we now know that the board should have invested in a full search and it should have hired the best candidate for the position. We might joke about qualifications yet when results are factored in several years down the road, often it is clear that hiring an inferior person often delivers inferior results. So, what are the qualifications to be a superintendent?

When Dr. Holodick went to Colorado State University, he learned the answer. The school gave him the following criteria but first they gave him a jar of marbles like so: It says on the front of the jar above in gold letters Colorado State University. Every three-credit course completed the Department Dean would remove a marble. When you lost all your marbles you were declared a superintendent of schools. In Pa. you must have at least a master's degree, and take specified course work, i.e. school law among many. In Luzerne County, a father on the board, now or previously, and a daddy-in-law who is a Pa. State Representative. Helps in the selection process but it should not.

Michael Buffer, Citizens Voice (local paper) reporter had labeled Brian Costello as the boyish looking superintendent. Costello continually validates the look by boyish (childish) behavior. Michael Buffer again outdid himself in labeling the WBASD Superintendent. In one of his headlines, Buffer stated "the super conducted tours of Mackin." He called him *the super*. Shortly after that headline, there were barbs showing superman with "little Brian's head superimposed."

Lack of respect for sure. It was not my idea but one cannot deny that it is a great way of having somebody else paint your adversary. Make no mistake about it folks, Brian Costello is not on the people's side in the battle of the Big Toxic School. All is fair in love and war. Thank you Citizens Voice. Thank you Michael Buffer. You and your paper made Brian Costello an easily identifiable man. Costello is not a victim; he is a beneficiary of a system that could be better.

Chances are if a school board is accustomed to hiring relatives using a board member *pick vote*, they will also hire their superintendent that way as they have a de facto practice of ignoring candidate's credentials and using relatives or friends' acclamation as in a he said, she said board voice acclamation. A pick vote, by the way is a method in which qualifications of potential new hires be damned. For many years, Board members would abstain when their favorite candidate would be voted upon but they would get their turn to pick the next hire one out of eight times.

It is a known fact that candidates for jobs in WBASD, do not have a chance unless they know a board member. At the hiring board meeting, board members bring up candidates' names they favor and the board votes them in. The board takes turns selecting the next hire. This is known as a pick-vote. It is a system designed to make sure the district gets only inferior new hires. No wonder the district has such poor results compared to others in the state. Did the pick vote pick the Big Toxic School site?.

Was Brian Costello a product of WBASB nepotism? Would they have dared select him using a pick vote? Everybody, they say, in the whole area liked Owen Costello, the current Superintendent's dad, but that is not the point. The senior Costello was most certainly a respected WBASD Board member for 16 years. Moreover, he was very pleased that his son Brian James Costello, the current WBASB Superintendent was appointed prior to his gaining the top position as the Director of Curriculum and Instruction for the District.

Nobody is now saying Owen Costello did not earn his board position. Nobody said that Costello Sr. or junior got their jobs because of nepotism but the relationship sure positioned the younger Costello in the district as one of a "ruling family." As noted above, in Luzerne Country, a father on the board, now or previously, such as Owen Costello and a daddy-in-law who is a Pa. State Representative, such as The Honorable Eddie Day Pashinsky, can pull a lot of power. Having two such important people vouching for one candidate doubles the candidate's chances.

For example, it may mean that less competent people can get top positions in the district. But, who knows if that happened in Costello's case?

The traditional employment of a person who never held the position of assistant superintendent or superintendent would typically mean that the individual would start for a lower salary and be given a three year "trial" contract." Yet, if favoritism is in play, the board might be inclined to start a person at a higher salary even though the board can bring in a neophyte employee for lots less of an impact on the taxpayers. What does this say for Little Brian Costello?

He clearly started at the highest salary ever paid in the WBASD and was awarded a five-year permanent contract—no trial run. How did that happen? Why not a lower salary and why not a typical three year test contract? Costello is the "super." For sure. He is also the boyish looking superintendent. Those who know him say he is a fine person.

When you think of the word boyish, childish may also come to mind. Please think about the super's vendetta against the entire City of Wilkes-Barre, which played a big role in the Big Toxic School's location on a contaminated mountain top. When he was appointed superintendent as the youngest superintendent ever in the district, it was the equivalent of voice acclamation. It was a given as some have noted.

There was the formality of a token search but some say it was not a real search. Ask yourself again if a national search for such a top position can be considered " paying the Pa. School Boards Association $10,000 to conduct the search" Would this be a "formal search?" Not in the minds of many people who know. Check out the published results in the beginning of this chapter.

Is it not hard to believe that somebody coming from a superintendent position in another district could not out-match the scant experience of Brian Costello. However, neither Dr. Holodick nor Brian Kelly nor anybody we knew got to ask any questions on the matter. All we can say is" How did that work out with the district going straight to the bottom in achievement rankings in the state. ? Here we are four years later #443 out of 501 in the state and almost one Big Toxic School to show for it.

Will the "super" make it to the end of his five year contract? Does he deserve it?. The bottom line is that there had not been an extensive search. Brian Costello was unanimously appointed district superintendent during a normal "pick vote" at a Tuesday school board meeting at the Solomon/Plains Junior High School in Plains Township. He took over when Bernard Prevuznak stepped down on September 1, 2016.

Besides his dad who served as board member, Brian James Costello had some family members who worked for the District. For example, his wife was an elementary teacher in WBASD. Whether he needed it or not, to help get the 8-0 unanimous vote of the board for the position, Brian James had some spare political connections.

On Sept 1, 2016, Costello got a full promotion from his Curriculum Manager job to Superintendent and his salary became $148,526. It was the highest salary in the District for one of the youngest employees. It had taken Prevuznak 35 years to make his grade by 2016. The average School Superintendent salary in Pennsylvania is $162,326 as of June 28, 2020, but the range typically falls between $132,605 and $195,880.

Reading School District – Nepotism???

Nepotism and Cronyism are complaints in many PA school districts besides the Wilkes-Barre Area School District (WBASD). Let us tell a quick story about the Reading School District. In this Pennsylvania community, it has almost become a mantra: "It's all about who you know." While school leaders deny its existence, there is a pervasive perception that the district is wrought with nepotism.

Many current and potential employees have the idea that friends and family members of school board members and administrators benefit unfairly because of their ties to school leaders. Based on information provided by the district, 28 of 2,200 district employees are related to board members who have served in the past two years. Dozens of other district employees are noted as friends of board members.

J. Drue Miles, who served as acting superintendent, said nepotism is a dark cloud hanging over the district. No wonder Wilkes-Barre Area sees it as a natural thing. There's an overabundant or uncommon amount of board members' relatives that are employed by the district," he said. And that, he said, impacts how the district operates.

"Absolutely, it certainly made our job, or the job of any administrator, much tougher," he said. He said some topics or issues were changed, put on hold or simply avoided because they would impact friends or relatives of board members. One such instance was the decision to close the district over Christmas break, which gave employees, including family and friends of board members, extra days off. The issue of nepotism was a recurring theme during hearings in September 2010 and February 2011 by the Pennsylvania Human Relations Commission.

"Some prospective, current and past district employees perceive that nepotism negatively impacts recruitment, employment and retention decisions," according to a report created by the commission following the hearings. The report notes that several witnesses at the hearings charged the district with nepotism.

Favoritism denied—when asked about nepotism, most school board members didn't shy away from the fact that they have friends and family working in the district. But they disputed accusations of favoritism.

Former board member John P. Santoro Jr., whose district records show that he had three family members working in the district, declined to discuss how many of his friends and relatives were employed by the district. But, he said, he considers a lot of district employees to be his friends.

"If you're talking friends, that list might be more like 100 because I have a lot of friends," Santoro said. "That doesn't mean I got them their jobs. I was on the board for 16 years; of course I'm going to have friends and know people who work for the district." Other board members shared similar sentiments, saying that just because people they know work in the district doesn't mean they didn't get their jobs fair and square.

Current board member Harry P. Storch Jr. said one of the names on the list, Wendy Moll, is his daughter. "She retired in November after 38 years as a teacher," Storch said. "She worked there long before I ever thought of running for the school board. How is that nepotism?" Storch also acknowledged that his son, Michael Moll, is an electrician employed in the district maintenance department.

"These are all highly qualified teachers," Storch said. "A teacher has to go to four years of college and then get a teaching certificate. An electrician has to be trained and certified by the state."

"Board members can't unilaterally hire district employees," Storch said. "You have to have five votes or you're screwed," he said.

Qualifications defended—Current Reading board member Pierre V. Cooper said his wife, her two sisters and a brother-in-law are employed by the district and are all highly qualified for the jobs they do. Their jobs include two education assistants, a teacher and a custodian. Cooper said he also had a niece who was briefly employed as a security guard.

Current board member Isamac Torres-Figueroa said her mother and sister are employed by the district but were hired before she was elected to the board. Former board members Keith R. Stamm and Joseph R. Breton and current board member Robert F. Heebner Jr. did not return calls seeking comment.

Current Reading board member Karen H. McCree said she has one daughter working for the district and knows many other people who work for the district. "One of the people I know got laid off last year, so if I'm using my influence to get people hired I'm not doing a very good job of it," McCree said.

She accused Miles of stirring up trouble. "It sounds to me like Mr. Miles should find better things to do with his time." But despite board members' assurances, those around the district aren't convinced everything is on the up and up. "I believe there are signs that would point to the existence or appearance of nepotism," said Bryan Sanguinito, president of the district's teachers' union. "Whether or not it truly exists, that is the perception." Sanguinito said that, particularly with the district facing the possibilities of layoffs, it is important for the school board to be transparent and fair.

"We need to make sure the process is done fairly," he said. "I have great faith in the school board that it will be done fairly."

Contact David Mekeel: 610-371-5014 or mekeel@readingeagle.com.

Do we know the WBASD hiring policy? Nepotism? Wilkes-Barre Area has no hiring policy that can be found though there have been some documented attempts to create one over the years. This became a big issue after the first of two board members were federally indicted in a pay-to-teach scheme where a prospective teacher's family paid to secure her a job. Back then the policy was tacitly called "get your wallet out."

Such a lack of rules casts a shadow on the competency of teachers, administrators, and even superintendents when nepotism is excused and pay for play rules are used to get jobs. How can the public expect competence in its employees when the board does not evaluate credentials?

"It is not fair to the kids who have graduated 30 years ago with my older daughters that are teachers and teaching in Maryland, Georgia, Florida, all over but here because they don't know the right people. And that's not fair. It should be strictly on merit and it never was," said Heights resident Susan Gilbert.

To demonstrate the brazenness of the WBASB, regarding the possibility of nepotism policies, on June 20, 2015, the Times Leader printed an article titled: *Zeroing In. Nepotism Alive and Well at Wilkes-Barre Area CTC*. The on/again off/again nepotism policy was off again.

Fresh off their unpopular votes to close Meyers High School, spending about $100 million to build a new school at Coughlin and not allowing the public to have a say about the matter in November's election, two Wilkes-Barre Area School Board members once again demonstrated they will do as they please. What pleased them Monday night was hiring a few more relatives. You GOTTA be kidding, you say. Why be surprised when this was simply business as usual for this group?

Remember the nepotism policy the Wilkes-Barre Area Career and Technical Center's joint operating committee discussed back in February? It's obviously still on the back burner collecting dust. But with good reason. Board member John Quinn, one of WBA's representatives on the CTC board, said in March that any such policy this board passes must be done right.

So meanwhile, with no obstacle blocking its path, the CTC board voted to hire the niece of Louis Elmy and the daughter-in-law of Ned Evans. Elmy and Evans both represent WBA on the CTC board.

Business as usual. Both directors are also kind of shameless. And so is the rest of the board's WBA contingent, Denise Thomas and Quinn, who voted for both hirings, and James Susek, who voted only for Elmy's niece. Don't they see or care how the public they just snubbed in their home district perceives this? Elmy and Evans didn't vote for their relatives because they can't. So, they abstained.

But it is apparently acceptable for a board member to make the motion to hire his kin because Elmy, the personnel committee chairman, did just that. He wasn't at the meeting but participated via a conference call, the Times Leader reported. So after he got the ball rolling, his fellow board members did the rest. And that's the way it's done at this school.

Crestwood School District representative Gene Mancini, who in March brought up the preposterous idea of implementing a nepotism policy at a school where nepotism reigns supreme, said he asked for an update at the April meeting. He said Quinn first corrected him that it was a hiring policy not a nepotism policy that was being considered. Then he informed him a board committee was discussing it. Now don't laugh, but Ned Evans, who's daughter-in-law was hired Monday, is on that committee. So we're guessing nepotism isn't a very big concern of his.

Regarding the job Elmy's niece, Samantha Elmy, got, administrative director Frank Majikes reassured everyone that she was the only candidate who applied for the newly-created $32,000 position of child care group assistant. He also said the job was advertised "all over." So what's a board to do? Obviously be thankful that at least a board member's relative wanted it. As for Evans' daughter-in-law Nicole Stella, Majikes said she was the best qualified candidate out of four or five interviewed for the $15.72 per hour custodian job.

He didn't need to tell us that. It's a given that when there's competition, more often than not, the most qualified candidate just happens to be related to a school director. This was in the local papers when Brian Costello was announced as the superintendent of schools for Wilkes-Barre Area School District.

FYI, when Costello was appointed superintendent by the board, the previous superintendent had praise for Mr. Costello. "He has been a very loyal and very good assistant," Prevuznak said of Costello. "He has had opportunity and has, very honestly, been recruited by other school districts to be their superintendent. He has a deep affection for this district, our employees and our students." So dedicated to this district he lives in Mountain Top, and his children and taxes go to Crestwood. We are so lucky!

Our thanks to the citizens voice as parts of this chapter were contributed by mbuffer@citizensvoice.com

Chapter 16 Is There Credibility in the WBA School Board?

Reported Failures in Competence, Morality and Legality.

If we had the criminal goods on the board, we would not have written three books to make our point. We would have gone to the FBI or whoever the proper authorities might well be. We have contacted the Luzerne Country DA for help in investigating the suppositions, suspicions, about the possibilities of corruption and wrong-doing in the management of the WBA school district.

But, I am sure you know folks, just because if it looks like a duck, and if it quacks it is typically a duck, does not mean that your authors have definitive proof that there was anything corrupt or untoward in the Big Toxic School project or any of the other decisions brought forth by the WBA School Board. We just have no evidence either way. Logical conclusions would suggest that some place there is a pile of cash to find this chicanery but we do not know for sure.

We need lawyers on the people's side and officials that oversee school boards in PA to check on this matter which the people of the

WB Area believe is suspicious. Writing about our suspicions may help us find advocates and sponsors to help the people make this situation better. Dr. Richard Holodick and Brian Kelly are not financially endowed enough to help the people of the WB Area so we offer our thoughts hoping there are some people with resources who like Coughlin, GAR, and Meyers and who would support SOS in an investigation to find the truth.

When you read the next section, you may be convinced that there are a number of nefarious characters who serve or who have served in various capacities on the Wilkes-Barre Area School Board. Nobody really wants to take credit for this section of this chapter slangly titled Credibility so let's say that somebody called Citizen Reporter provided all of this information to us today

Credibility of the WBA School Board.

If we were not trying to figure out how any school board could determine that it was prudent to destroy three beautiful community high schools in Wilkes-Barre City and replace them with a monstrous consolidated toxic school built on a hazardous waste dump, perhaps this chapter in this book would not have been necessary.

The people are asking and have been asking: "What board would do such a thing to Wilkes-Barre Area residents?" The answer is the same board that would do the deeds highlighted in the below headlines and detailed in the following paragraphs. We wish this were not true and that it did not have to be in this book. But, how else can we explain the types of characters who have existed in this School Board otherwise? Know that they have voted to undermine an entire city and its surrounding areas for no good reason. Nonetheless they did!

HEADLINES:

- W-B Area Keeps Pizzella as President
- Former W-B Area Board President Faces Life in Prison
- Truth will set (President) Height free sooner
- Second WBA Director (President Thomas) in Hot Water

This board majority either doesn't know or doesn't care about the perceptions of the public regarding neglect in basic maintenance of facilities.

Many do not know that Geisinger Hospital offered the Board 55 acres free and the board rejected it. I do not recall hearing a board opinion on this? Then, there was the lack of a second opinion on historic Meyers High School. Why not?

Instead the board put a big X on Meyers High School despite its architectural elegance, and despite cautions by community groups decided to build a public school on a coal ash, toxic dump. The board also decided to employ contract services based on the size of the wallet or connections of the contractor.

By the way, this is an exact quote from Auditor General Schapiro. His quote memorialized the thought process relating to DEP, WBA's watch dog on the toxic dump site upon which the board decided to set sail (build its consolidated Taj Mahal). If it is such a good idea why would the people of WB Area nickname the project as The Big Toxic School. Will these people enroll their children in a school that offers them the opposite of clean air and clean water?

At a board meeting Dr. Prevuznak the prior superintendent made the statement, "we can't do this alone we need your help." It is a long story that we make short by telling the reader that Save Our Schools (SOS) was formed and spent 4 years plus trying to assist the board—the WBASB, whose president / board facility chair considered this community group as adversaries.

He told the SOS President, Dr. Richard Holodick "you have a choice—SOS or the board." Mr Caffery rejected other qualified people for the external task force because they have plans. Upon examination all who examined their plans say that it speaks volumes compared to the "no plan" approach of the WBASB. We have outlined a lot of problems with the Wilkes-Barre Area School District in this two-volume book set in addition to the board's character flaws brought out in the credibility section in this chapter.

We have said this before but we must repeat. The problem is the board. Yes, there is one major cause for all the problems the School

District faces—Bad management. We might add that it appears that the management board and superintendent are not heavy on the caring part also. So, they make bad decisions and they do not care who those decisions hurt. You may be able to count as high as ten fingers but you won't find more than one source for persistent problems. It is management—in other words, in WBASD, it is the WBASB.

When a company puts out a bum product or has a bad marketing program or regularly hires incompetent people, who can we blame? Right! It is the company's or the organization's management. Blame top management. Any problem that any organization suffers theoretically could have been overcome by excellent managers. You don't get to hire excellent managers however by using poor judgment and techniques such as favoritism, patronage, nepotism, and cronyism. See the last chapter for further details about the history of hiring new employees at WBA.

Superintendents are clearly highly visible actors in the American education system. As the highest ranking official in a school district, the superintendent receives a lot of credit when things go well, and just as much blame when they don't. In most areas of the state, a school district superintendent is largely a short-term job. The typical superintendent has been in the job for three to four years. It is unusual for a superintendent with poor results to last more than three or four years.

And, so, it just happens that the WBA Superintendent Costello will have completed four years in his position on September 1, 2020. With our academic achievement one of the lowest ranked in the state, and the Big Toxic School, becoming an embarrassment to the area, should we expect the current young superintendent to outlast the norm? Will he seek a better job where he is not known—out of the area? Who knows?

If he looks for retention, what notable successes do you think that a retention contract would cite? When things blow up in a business or in a school district despite management taking some action it is because the organization happens to have bad managers, poor managers, or OK, let's call it what they are—incompetent managers.

It is what it is and it will never change in any organization unless or until there is a management change for the better.

Rest assured, everything that goes wrong in any organization is top management's fault. In a school district, that would mean it is the superintendent's fault unless the board recognizes it. Since the board can fire the superintendent if they see incompetence and do not act, it would in this case, be the board's fault. So as we dissect the problems which come to the surface rapidly when we examine Wilkes-Barre School District, knowing what we now know, are they all unsolvable if they ever were? Not if we are willing to excise bad management from the scenario.

Looking at the outside barometers and thermometers that we see when we compare the district against others in the state of PA, do we find any problems? In a recent "contest". When we looked at the school districts in various categories, and there are about 501 or more in the state, we found Wilkes-Barre Area hugging the bottom at a lofty 443 out of the 501. If you lived in WBA and Brian Costello were your superintendent, and you had a vote, would you recommend him for a bonus or for remedial training?

It sure seems that this district is at the bottom of everything in area school district categories. The WBASB outlined a new venture in 2014 titled Pathway to the Future. Just like a lot of the initiatives the board sets forth; they did not bring on the right horses to carry the heavy project load. For example the implementers simply did / do not have the experience to pull off the plan. What is the problem?

1. Seriously Inexperienced Superintendent
2. Four Architect firms with zero experience in large school restoration& sparse experience in large school construction.

Other killers of the Pathway's progress included the fact that the board chose to ignore / bypass its own internal and external task force committees. Moreover, one of its own board members was motivated to write an alternate plan of action. Also, he "publicly" requested the board take time out (moratorium) to get more information.

Not only is the Pathway team steering a sinking ship. It has brought the ship to the bottom academically and near the bottom in attendance. Consolidation as a goal does not help matters. It is a proven method to work if the goal is to reduce academic achievement.

A big school will further reduce attendance. Moreover, when bussing is added to this isolated, toxic, "arsenic-ridden" coal ash dump, subsidence prone site, things will get even worse We're right around the corner from doomsday. That's why Wilkes-Barre residents are enrolling in charter schools.

P.S. All other districts interviewed in the "contest" had responses from the superintendent. Our director responded also. He gave the excuse that WBA's poor showing was because of a 76% poverty rate and that the state cut the funding short by $33 million. Yet, despite blaming being broke, the same Superintendent spearheads the monster spending of a HALF BILLION DOLLARS for a monument on a toxic hill that serves only a third of the area students.

He was not been trying to save taxpayer dollars when he paid 5x the value of the land for the school. He also purchased 45 acres more than needed. He had two swimming pools, two-football stadiums, and 8 coach's offices for part-time coaches. What "impoverished" community could afford that??? He even spent a million dollars to expand the swimming pool for competitive events and we still can't host competitive events. And, the library is still way too small? Tell me please because I cannot figure it out. How does that accommodate a poverty-prone area?

The SOS group is always looking for some hope on the horizon regarding some authoritative body such as the PA Attorney General's Office or the PA Auditor General's Office or any official body to shut down the building of the Big Toxic School for the good of the people. Is anybody listening out there?

The Grand Jury investigating DEP on their oversight of fracking.

The Dept. of the Interior, Washington DC is looking into DEP oversight of mining across Pa. The Attorney General wisecracked that the oversight is dependent on the size of the wallet and Board connections. Not a funny joke! There are also issues with waterways and runoff concerns? The fact is, the WBASB has committed both malfeasance and misfeasance in office and they need to be shut down for these crimes against the people in areas in which they should have engaged but did not, the board committed non-feasance in office.

It sure would be nice if somebody from the state or the federal government would do their jobs and do the right thing.

We have explained this a number of times in this two-book set but here we go again to make sure officials in the state and federal government get it. Malfeasance in office or official misconduct is the commission of an unlawful act, done in an official capacity that affects the performance of official duties. This board could teach a graduate course in all forms of blank-feasance.

Malfeasance in office is often grounds for a just cause removal of an elected official by statute or a recall election. Malfeasance in office contrasts with" misfeasance in office," which is the commission of a lawful act done in an official capacity that improperly causes harm; and "nonfeasance in office," is the failure to perform an official duty. One word to describe the WBASB regarding all three mal, mis, and non-feasances in office—Guilty!

Nobody is giving up. For starters the SOS members of the Board will be making some basic common sense motions, even if they don't think they will pass. For example, there should be a motion to get a second opinion from restoration firms as to alternate uses for Meyers High School and costs. There should also be a district-wide study conducted of district employees, parents/guardians, and taxpayers.

Moreover, an RFP should be sought to develop a long-range curriculum/facility master plan. Why is there none now? Shouldn't the superintendent assure that one is followed? Quite frankly if most of the board chooses not to not go along with these very basic tools, it uncovers that there are hidden agendas. It would be time to get the hell off this board as it would be effective proof that the board is not supportive of the people. And, there may be criminal acts and fraud involved.

Years back there was local news coverage considered "investigative reporting." Today it is tough to find publicity in the papers or the TV stations or the Radio Stations in NEP about some secret truths about the goings on machinations of this board. Not too many in the public domain trust what is happening. We need a spotlight on the malfeasance of this Board in the matter of the Big Toxic School built on an ugly mine-waste-contaminated site.

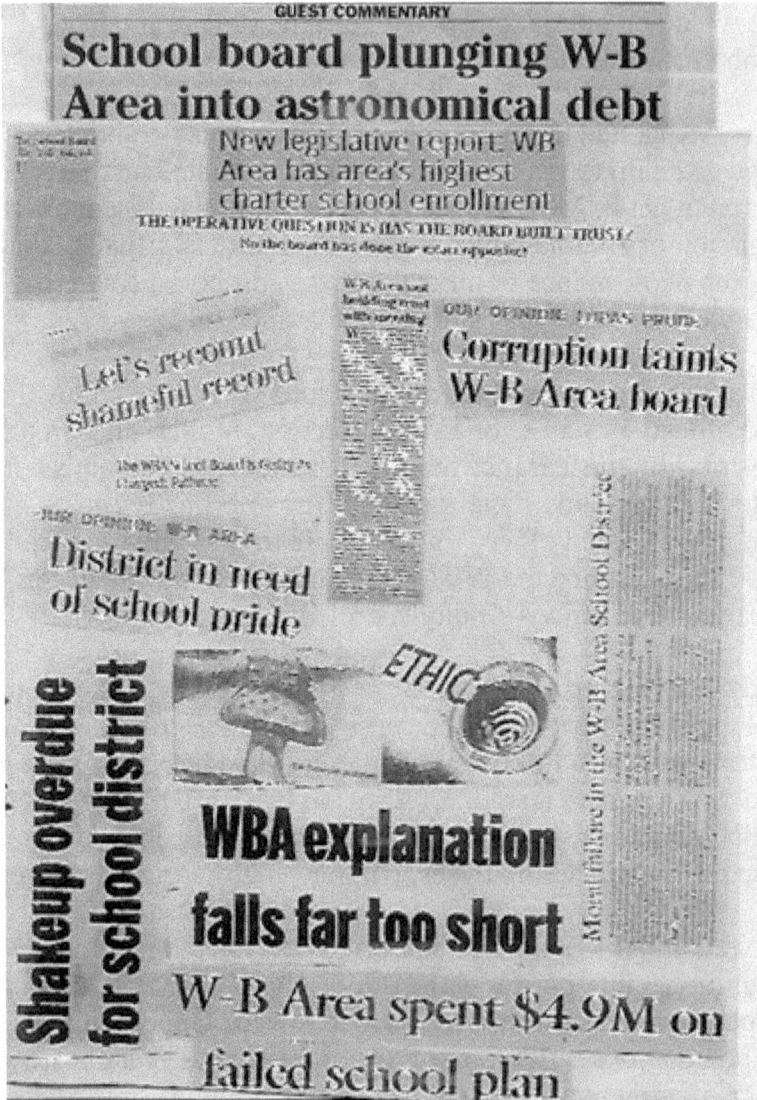

GUEST COMMENTARY

School board plunging W-B Area into astronomical debt

New legislative report: WB Area has area's highest charter school enrollment

THE OPERATIVE QUESTION IS: HAS THE BOARD BUILT TRUST? No the board has done the exact opposite!

Let's recount shameful record

OUR OPINION: IT WAS PRUDE

Corruption taints W-B Area board

OUR OPINION: W-B AREA **District in need of school pride**

ETHIC

Shakeup overdue for school district

WBA explanation falls far too short

W-B Area spent $4.9M on failed school plan

Perhaps Philly or Harrisburg, will spotlight what NEP chooses not to do. This sure is frustrating.

The board gets away with purchasing an un-reclaimed mining land and pays 5 times the assessed value. Why? This is in violation of their own board action, not to mention common sense and ethics. They begin work on the site exceeding a million dollars, for a site not owned by the district. And, the Auditor General conducts what is supposed to be a clean and honest audit and for his own reasons that do not resemble the truth, he praises the District for what might have been criminal acts.

The Board pays the Solicitor $19,000 a month? That is a lot of money. Why? In our presence, and the former super's, and the facility committee members, the solicitor said a zoning failure was impossible. He was assigned to negotiate the purchase. He convinced the board the property was worth $4.2 million based on mineral rights; mineral rights were not in the deeds. He must not have read the deeds? Who got the excess money? This is misfeasance in office.

Why is there no accountability?

It took a Back Mountain Realtor, who took the district to magistrate court to prove that there was something stinky in Dallas. Who paid for that? The Board's own solicitor convinced the board majority that the coal ash was safe as long as the students didn't dig down and actually eat the coal ash. How is that not malfeasance? (i.e. wrongdoing, especially by a public official)

This is all in the board minutes. Why did the Auditor General not find it? Nobody can tell a thinking person that none of the following applies to this board—the six who voted for The Big Toxic High.

They should be removed from office.

There is enough hard evidence to which names can be attached that demonstrate some really stupid decisions. It is a disappointment that it may be tough to validate a board member, who we know watched half naked women on his cell phone during a meeting (provable) and who reportedly ran a house of ill-repute. What about a board member who referred to students as MooMoo's—a board member???.

And there was another comment so gross we can't type it, in reference to young children of color. Summarize this paragraph with an inexperienced superintendent being paid a full salary; No in-house facilities expertise; four inexperienced architect firms selected by the superintendent who were charged with the restoration activities. Was somebody trying to assure a high-cost failure?

How about the egregious untoward replacement of a board member using past nepotistic practices ahead of 15 outstanding dedicated applicants. How about this new member being a basketball coach/teacher whose children were not in the District—instead they were in a private school and the newly appointed board member had never attended a WBA board meeting. Somehow nepotism worked in the past as his brother was on the board and his wife was appointed as a district teacher while nepotism was seemingly in play.

Summary of the public's grievances v the board

- Academic failure, highest dropout rate in the state fleeing to cyber and charter schools, highest truancy in the state, ranked 444th out of 501 school districts in state testing.
- Poverty levels of the district residents, students, and fiscal condition of the school district. The half-billion-dollar project with no master plan, and an outlandish expenditure for a third of the students, leaving 4500 students and six other aged facilities deficits. Zero impact studies prior to board actions.
- History of board members fraud and FBI indictments.
- Moral & Morale decay in the district.
- Nepotism, cronyism, and employing and contracting with the inexperienced.
- Gross neglect of three historic high schools, failing due diligence in restoration efforts.
- Racism
- Site selection & failure to assess property value resulting in a gross overpayment.
- Questionable site purchasing procedure.
- Consolidation, reasons for consolidation, and results of consolidation in other districts.
- Apparent emphasis on sports.
- Impact potential removing all high schools from the city.
- Profile of board members legal and moral issues. Board intimidation tactics.
- Ignoring community input, major agencies, PDE, PSBA, AIA, and Pa. Historical Society, scholarly research, their own facility study, and state sponsored PFM financial study.

- Ignoring five other states that prohibit public schools NEAR contaminated sites,

WBA builds on top of a contaminated site

How about this story, where did the money go, and on the same page left bottom, "Former W-B board President faces life in prison." This was at a time when major costly decisions were made by a convicted extortionist, along with a few other impaired board members. It was reported that $10 million dollars was spent over the approved operational budget.

Here are a bunch of firsts for WBASD.

- The employment of a superintendent with zero experience at the assistant or superintendent levels; past administrative experience 4 years as an assistant principal (student discipline); 4 years in the central office as director of curriculum, responsible for student's academic achievement. How did that work? District ranked 433/501 in state

- The traditional three-year contract for novice superintendent, ignored—awarded a 5-year contract. Supposedly un related to his dad a previous board member, or his father-in-law a state representative.

- Starting salary, $148,000, the salary it took the previous superintendent with massive experience including assistant superintendent, over 20 years to reach.

- Board member, with an apparent alcohol abuse problem, posted on social media the humor in an Az Teacher having oral sex with a student. So gross we will not type it, so egregious 8 board members and the superintendent requested his resignation. He would not resign and still is on the board.

- A former district clerk elected to the board had 13 e-mails found on her school district computer that were racist and put down disadvantaged children; claimed someone else used her computer when she was on break.

- She was elected to the board presidency, and vice president at a time when the board was desperate for experienced leadership.

- Headline 2nd board member in hot water. Her posts on social media add to the probability of her sending the racial e-mails.

- Former board president Elmy facing a life sentence. • FBI indicted board member elected board president a short time AFTER the indictment.

So much for credibility!

Chapter 17 A Small, Ethically Strong, Family-Oriented, Poverty Level City Deteriorates

Life in the new WBASD is unhealthy— educationally, financially, and facility-wise.

Most of he information in this chapter has also been included in Book 1 of the two book set.

In a small senior populated city, operating below the poverty level, with its share of corruption at high levels, including the "Kids for Cash" scandal, another unsavory story has come under the scrutiny of the light of day. It began with a recalcitrant school board using its maintenance neglected high schools as an excuse for an unjustifiable high school consolidation and the best football class (6A) for HS football. This all has morphed into a community's struggle to assure input, adherence to educational principals, fiscal responsibility, and now, the very health of its children.

Without a master plan, community dialogue and outreach, or siting tools for schools such as those provided by the EPA, and after throwing away $6 million on a site that was destined not to receive zoning approval, the school board selected the worst possible parcel of land this side of a failed nuclear plant. They plan to put about 2500 students on this site, which has limited access and no infrastructure per se, with no pedestrian access. The site will require 95-100% busing while the existing constituent schools allowed 65-70% of students to walk.

The land's former uses are nothing less than scary/ It was first deep coal mined, then surface mined with huge culm banks dotting the landscape. It then put as shift in of ten years as an unlined toxic coal ash landfill. It look like nothing is close by, yet. There is a major expressway with major air pollution potential just a "stone's throw" away. The board of directors' remediation plan, "cap in place," is inferior to coal ash removal and. In places, it will mean less than a foot of soil can be obtained from the site, a site which looks much like the city of Pripyat the nearest town to the power plant at Chernobyl. Believe us please--that is bad!.

The stats on poisonous substance at the top of the mountain should have precluded anything ever being built there. Why would an board bypass reason and select such a poor site? There is a litany of reasons why not to build there, and no reasons to forge ahead.

Consider first that arsenic in the soil exceeds permissible concentrations for residential use. There has been no assay for expected and toxic hexavalent chromium or uranium decay products that are common in ash. If the public could take a huge wooden spoon and mix this panoply of carcinogens in a huge mixing bowl of carcinogens, it would deliver more truth than exaggeration and it would be just the beginning. Five states are so concerned for their children that they would not permit a school even near such toxic coal ash. The EPA has opined that ash is a health risk greater than smoking.

We have the evidence. Of 900 workers who had intimate and daily contact with coal ash after a pond spill in Tennessee just ten years ago, 43 are dead and 300 are sick or dying. The public in Wilkes-Barre Area ask the School Board how they could think such a site is good for students and teachers and others to pollute their lungs with the debris from years of accumulated contamination. How could this site, known for its toxicity have even been considered, let alone selected.

Industry experts concluded years ago that the disposal of coal combustion waste in coal mines is poisoning to streams and drinking water supplies across the country. The solid waste generated by burning coal in power plants (the type of waste in the Big Toxic School site) is the second largest industrial waste stream in the United States. In fact, enough coal combustion waste (CCW) is generated each year in the United States to fill a train stretching from Washington, D.C. to Melbourne, Australia.

With no federal standards for disposal of coal combustion waste, more commonly referred to as coal ash, companies often dump it in locations that allow numerous toxic constituents to leach, or dissolve, out of the waste and into nearby streams, ponds, rivers, lakes and other waters. From New Mexico to North Carolina, on up through Pennsylvania, water contaminated by coal combustion waste has poisoned communities and killed fish and livestock.

In December 2008, for a representative example. a dike constructed of ash for a coal ash sludge impoundment failed at the Tennessee Valley Authority's Kingston Fossil Plant in Harriman, Tennessee. Think of the magnitude of this failure in a site that for years was studied for its greatness in every grade school and high school in the nation. For years, students learned that the most successful New Deal program created by President Franklin D. Roosevelt was the Tennessee Valley Authority (TVA). The TVA was successful in decentralizing power and control and increasing the standard of living for the inhabitants of the southeastern United States (US).

The EPA unfortunately takes building a school for 2200+ children in a remote burg in Plains Twp. PA on top of a toxic mine dump a bit too lightly simply because nobody in the country knows about it. That is going to change because of this book and other tell-all's like it. The EPA may very well react to the squeaky wheel as in all things in life, the big squeaky wheel gets the most grease.

The TVA, a big fish in a big pond, literally could not hide away out of sight. And so when independent fish sampling results found high levels of toxic chemicals in Kingston, TN, fly ash deposits and Emory River fish on 5-18-09, the EPA was forced to take action to ameliorate the public. Let's hope the pattern continues with the Big Toxic School Pennsylvania incident. So far Pennsylvania's DEP has taken no action. They are asleep at the switch.

Preliminary analyses of ash, water, sediments, and fish tissues collected near the TVA spill site 18 days following the dike failure revealed the following:

1) the total recoverable toxic elements arsenic, barium, cadmium, lead, and selenium in water exceeded protective drinking water and/or aquatic life criteria levels;

2) ash and ash-laden river sediments had arsenic levels that exceeded the EPA removal limits; selenium levels increased dramatically downstream of the spill;

3) selenium levels in fish were at and beyond the thresholds of toxicity for reproduction and growth;

4) fish suffered internal and external impacts from the spill, with abnormal changes to gills in particular;

5) detailed analysis of floating ash particles (cenospheres) found that approximately 10% of these particles contain an iron oxide coating that may be transporting arsenic into water.

Think of the damage to 2200 kids breathing in toxic ash fumes with nobody monitoring their health in Plains TWP's own Big Toxic School site. How are we even to judge who needs assistance and how will they receive it when despite the poisonous evidence, the state of PA's DEP and the EPA says all is OK? They know the issues but they think that by being silent, they can save the effort. Northeastern PA must not be an area on their important list.

The TVA failure was massive. It caused the release of over 1 billion gallons of toxic coal ash sludge over 300 acres, poisoning streams and rivers with unsafe amounts of arsenic, lead, chromium, thallium, and other toxic metals. That's the stuff the school building in Plains Twp. and all 100+ acres exposes.

Help for Wilkes-Barre Area please.

Despite the risk of life-threatening disasters like the one that occurred in Tennessee, and the extensive, documented damage to human health and the environment by coal ash throughout the U.S., there are still no specific federal regulations governing the disposal of this waste. When the Save Our Schools group alerted the DEP and the EPA, it was looked upon as a lesser event than a voice crying out in a desert. It was ignored like as if kids breathing carcinogens in NEPA does not matter. Local and state and federal corrupt politics prevailed. The people be damned. The biggest risk for authorities seemed to be that if corrective action was taken, the wallet of somebody important would not grow.

In the absence of federal regulations, many states continue to allow dumping of coal ash into unlined mine pits, where the waste's toxic constituents can migrate unimpeded into groundwater. Dumping coal combustion waste into mines is especially dangerous because mining often creates conditions that allow for more rapid contamination of adjacent groundwater. Based on mine disposal rates in Pennsylvania, West Virginia, Indiana, Ohio, Illinois, Texas, North Dakota, and New Mexico, plus conservative estimates of mine disposal in seven other coal basin states, it has been estimated that approximately 24 to 25 million tons of CCW, or 20 percent of generation, are mine filled each year.

Under these conditions, the waste's toxic contaminants, including arsenic, cadmium, chromium, lead, selenium and thallium, can readily pollute streams and drinking water. This is both scary and dangerous for the people. The disturbed land in this toxic dump from the building of the Big Toxic School on the top of a mountain with housing developments built on the way up the mountain is already polluting residences and will go on polluting for years to come after the big concrete toxic school complex and the big football stadium is built and the residents either move out or are deceased from the poisonous runoff. Not a pretty thought. But true, nonetheless.

The DEP and the EPA if interested enough to stop this travesty could prove for the students, teachers, workers, and residents that these chemicals can result in a number of health effects in humans, including neurological damage, cancer, and reproductive failure, as well as widespread ecosystem damage. Why let this scourge happen? If the SOS group had the funding, you can bet like Erin Brockavich, there would be a big lawsuit.

The DEP and the EPA have big pocketbooks and nonetheless the Big Toxic School remediation plan is not on their to-do-list.

Federal regulations and Federal action in Plains Twp. were needed to ensure that essential safeguards were in place before coal combustion waste was disposed of in coal mines. But, safety was and continues to be ignored. These safeguards would have ensured that companies would reveal the toxicity of the waste they are dumping, identify sources of groundwater and surface water that are susceptible to contamination from the dumping, and prohibit the disposal of waste directly into groundwater. Surely nobody in their right mind would permit over $120 million to be spent on a school for over 2000 students who would be breathing pollutants every day and drinking polluted water.

The WBASB was made aware of the problems but they denied their possibility despite the facts. Federal regulations should have required long-term, comprehensive monitoring for pollution from the dumping, and ensure that mine owners were held financially responsible for cleanup—especially when the intended use of the site is a school complex. What could be more serious?

Because state regulations uniformly fail to require these safeguards, the U.S. Environmental Protection Agency must immediately act to establish federal minimum standards that ensure full protection of human health and the environment in coalfield communities. SOS suggests that the Big Toxic School be the test case and the testing should begin immediately—right after a cease-and-desist order is issued for the completion of the school. If anybody out there can afford the justice needed, please contact Dr. Richard Holodick, save our Schools President, and he will immediately make you one of the team.

Environmental jurisdiction and assistance for concerned citizens is muddled: EPA is the only agency with a coal ash rule which includes guidance on shutting down landfills, but they have no jurisdiction on mining land. The Office of Surface Mining of the Department of Interior, has not yet formulated a coal ash rule. Traditionally, these entities defer to the state, anyway. Pennsylvania's DEP involvement is split between two offices, is mining friendly, and is very interested in re-purposing scarred mining land. That's laudable, but not this land for this purpose.

Adding to the mystery, the land was assessed between $200,000 and $800,000 but purchased from the mining company of dubious background, for $4.2 million. Why? The mining permit is still active and held by that company, and the bond ensuring land reclamation which ordinarily predates sale, is still held by the mining company. Despite that, the district's contractors have been busily "compacting" the site at public expense, that is, doing the reclamation work of Pagnotti Enterprises on the WBASD dime.

Adding to the concern is the behavior of capped heavy metals and ash too near the Susquehanna River which is about 400 meters downgrade from this site. It serves as a drinking water source for distant communities and is the Chesapeake Bay's largest tributary. There is the potential for leaching toxins. Neighbors have witnessed subsidence and sludge in yards since compaction began; an orange trail is visible via Google Earth near the site and apparently extending to the river.

As citizens of the area, we are concerned about a chronic disease and cancer cluster at this site. Our board majority is not comprised of chemists. They have the same background as most of us. It begins and ends with a home chemistry kit as a child at best. Listening to the engineers they have retained for years, who seem to have a stake in the project, as well as DEP, which has said a lot but never once said the word, "safe," they press on, protesting the safety of thisdumping ground. Protests, letters, and public testimony have fallen on deaf ears. I hope authorities will choose to look into this. Representatives of Environmental Integrity Project have called this site "unprecedented." The Wilkes-Barre, Pa. community agrees. Perhaps some attention from an authoritative and neutral source might hold the feet of these arrogant pencil-pushers to the fire.

Chapter 18 Research, Planning, and Implementation

Submitted by Richard A. Holodick, Ph. D.

First, we must establish where we are in January 2021. It is vitally important. It is so important because in 2001, I retired from public education returning home to Luzerne County. My district was at the ground level of a demise second to none. It was then that I made a personal commitment to assist the Wilkes-Barre School District in its efforts to improve.

To this end, I began by writing a position paper. I presented this to the board president James Atherton, then an employee of the district. Looking back in history, you would discover that at that time the district had a cash surplus in excess of $15 million. Additionally, the students were ranked 144th out of 501 school districts in the state of PA.

That surplus is long gone. The PFM Inc. recently reported a potential $70 million dollar deficit. For all practical purposes this meant that two historic high schools would have to be demolished and replaced with a consolidated school built on the worst possible piece of toxic subsidence prone ground. The site was 124 square miles of pristine north eastern Pennsylvania land.

Neglect, denial, must cease! Today, three historic architecturally significant neighborhood high schools remain in question. However, the board has previously identified GAR High School to be used as a middle school. This, is in opposition to copious research on middle schools and the district's own facility study.

An impact study must be done for a GAR conversion/restoration when it could reach $40 million dollars with added bussing.

A properly executed impact study at the right time, would have saved the taxpayer millions of dollars with the Mackin School project. This was an attempt to put 800 students in a school designed for 500-students.

An impact study would have prevented the board's spending $3 million on pre-sale work and putting the building up for sale for less than $2 million netting a $million dollar loss.

The neglect of Meyers High School, and continual public statements on the how bad the building is, including the sheds, aka as theatrical props, are not positive to a facility the district wants to sell. Look at the props enshrouding the entrance like a slum addition to what is a very attractive school.

Very ugly Picture of Meyers High School Entrance With "Theatrical Props" What board in its right mind would do this to a high school?

For many years, the district has had in its possession a very good proposal to perform an evaluation of the facility for under $100,000. It was submitted by Bancroft out of Delaware. The restoration of the P.S. DuPont school shown above which used a proposal similar to Bancroft won many awards. The school is about the same size and age as Meyers. The difference unfortunately comes down to enlightened v unenlightened management.

Next, for your examination and consideration, is the consolidated high school. Because of a dispute with the City of Wilkes-Barre, the Superintendent told those who would hear that he would not build in Wilkes-Barre because they had dissed the district by not approving a zoning waiver. So, some say for spite, the superintendent found another site, This site is out of Wilkes-Barre City in Plains Twp. It is land that the state and the board's team have identified as a challenge upon which to build. Why? Could it be because of its poisonous contamination.

It is a former mine and toxic waste dump. The coal ash prevalent on the site produces toxins that must be capped, and the drainage consists of contaminated water that must be controlled and monitored due to runoff affecting residential dwelling and the proximity of the Susquehanna River that feeds the Chesapeake Bay.

The severity of these problems and the need for consistent monitoring may require an ongoing committee (task force). If the board insists on finishing this project, my suggestion is a committee chairperson such as Meyers graduate, former US government employee and member of the Penn State committee on environmental issues, Robin Shudak. The bottom line of course is that a written plan for observation and reporting is a requirement.

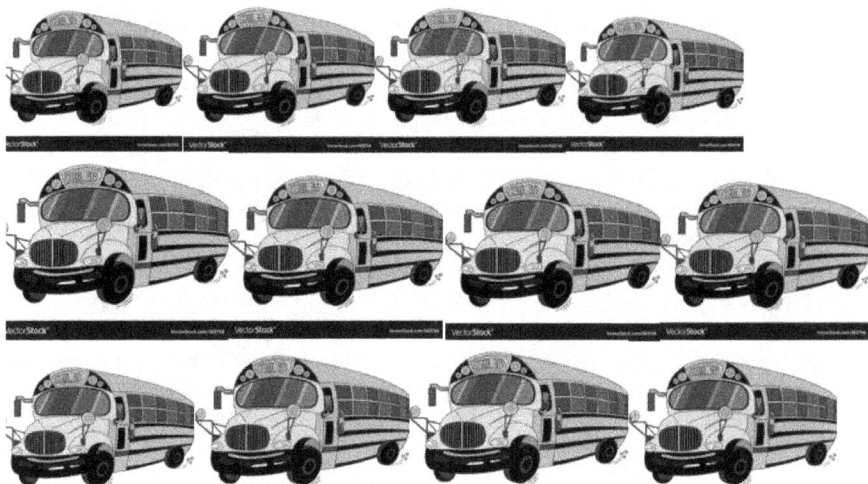

The school busses are an Illustration, point made, not quite. There are at least 10 more rows needed in the illustration to bus 2,000 students twice a day. Lots of busses for sure. I use the 60-bus need based on the ability to put 50 students in each buss.Not possible! Some buses will be full some with as little as ten students based on location and routes.

About 250 employee and students' cars 250 add to what must be managed. The 124 square mile site goes as far as Blakley Corners, with assigned pickup and drop off locations. It is a major challenge. This site, as shown in the aerial photo below and is positioned between River/Maffet Street and North Main Street. It does not take a transportation engineer to see the difficulty.

What is next, is equivalent to the transportation impact study which should have been done prior to the purchase of the site. When a district is proposing a half billion-dollar investment expecting it will improve the delivery of education, save the taxpayers money, address the aged facilities, as much data as possible must be sought.

As important as it is to support for any plan presented and implemented, nothing worthwhile happens over-night. All must be accommodated—support of faculty and staff because they will need to live with it; support of the taxpayers as they will have to pay for it.The proper process is to survey the stake holders.

Visiting those districts in like circumstances helps in evaluating choices. I visited the West Shore School District, Camp Hill Pennsylvania. They did not just begin to build. Instead, they performed a district wide survey that I recommend this board examine and follow. Like WBASD, this district also faced aged facilities and like most districts faced financial limitations.

The impact study, a re-assessment of Meyers, a conversion of GAR to a middle school, and a collection of opinions/recommendations from all stake holders must begin in January2021 for anything to work here. Why? Previous errors and omissions that in my opinion reach $20 million, and the fact that 4500 students and six more aged facilities will need to be addressed.

The information gathered will be the foundation for the mandated curriculum/facility long range master plan. This management tool omitted at the start of this building project was very costly resulting in some damage that is irreversible. The school board, based on the administration's assurance acts as if there is a master plan. Yet, there is none and has not been one. This fits the saying: "It's not what you know that will hurt you, it's what you know that ain't so that will hurt you."

A professionally produced master plan, could cost as much as $1 million but it would have already saved $20 million. It would have prevented closing a high school prematurely, It would have prevented the Mackin folly and the Kistler project, and the isolation of a public school akin to prisons, in a school that looks like it is built more as a correctional facility.

Master Plan w/credit to The Harrisburg Area Community College

I tried many times in one way or another; but I admit in dealing with this recalcitrant board, I have been unsuccessful in my attempts to get my message across to the board. It is as message about the right way to do things. It begins with the concept of a master curriculum and facility plan. I have been trying since 2001 to no avail. Check the board minutes.

When a school district has deplorable student achievement scores; when all facilities are not meeting state standards needing over a quarter of a billion dollars to meet those standards; and a district is fiscally in dire straits, a master plan short and long range is mandated. This board not only failed to execute a plan, it failed to plan.

Without a plan, the district has serious credibility problems. Coming out weekly with temporary plans like two million dollars for modular classrooms does not cut it. Nor does split schedules, buying an old building and retro fitting it as a school (Times Leader Bldg), especially with a costly lease of $55,000 a month.

When the construction began, as expected by yours truly, there were a ton of change orders. Spending one hundred million dollars to accommodate 2000 students with no organized plan for the other 5000 makes little to no sense.

In trying to convince the board to plan, I presented an RFP to develop a master plan that had been used for the Harrisburg Area Community College. It lays out in order of priority what the college was seeking in order to have a phased implementation plan over the next ten years. The was my second attempt at reality, the first was an extensive power point presentation of (A) what had to be done, (B) when it had to be done and (C) by whom. It was virtually ignored by the board. It became the reality of no plan.

The task force committees were a third effort of mine that failed. I have highlighted this to make it easier for you to read. The board scenario as recommended was to replace Coughlin in a residential area with adequate acreage. This would be accomplished by putting out an extensive RFP to have a master curriculum and facility plan developed. To do less for a potential three hundred-million-dollar project would affect the education of our children negatively, would promote management by crisis, would cause serious credibility problems with the taxpayers, and it would cause families to flee the district. This district is already in a crisis because of these moves. !

The Harrisburg RFP begins with a clearly stated PURPOSE. They seek a plan that establishes a framework for the orderly development of all capital improvements to support the role, mission and educational plans of the college.

The second paragraph addresses the need to identify funding sources for the project. In consideration of the value of master planning, the college will assure that the plan is updated every five years. They state, "the master plan will include:

- **A Comprehensive Environmental Scan**
- **An Academic Plan:**
- **A Comprehensive Facilities Assessment and**
- **A Strategic Facilities Implementation Plan.**

This paragraph pronounces it all. The establishment of **"EDUCATIONAL PLANS."** It is hard to understand how architects can begin the design of a facility without knowing the educational plans. It has been stated that the WBA district is following a comprehensive academic plan provided by the state. If so, that plan is not working according to the student test scores. Second, traditionally prior to the design of a facility the architects will confer with each teacher or department head to assist in the development of educational specifications. Where are the educational specifications here? They are woefully absent.

The second issue is to identify how the project(s) will be funded. This is done up front. Ask yourself how can architects design a facility without knowing the available budget? The design of a facility at a cost of eighty million dollars will look quite different than a two hundred million dollar facility. This most certainly held true as no budget limitation was established prior to the $443,000 facility study made by the four architectural firms on contract with the district. As we all know, this resulted in every recommendation adding up well past the hundred million dollar limit that was established after the study. This also resulted in a seriously flawed discriminatory plan submitted to PDE PlanCon. No lessons learned.

Another very important requirement of the Harrisburg community college RFP was the need to identify a Strategic Facilities Implementation Plan. The best the WBASB could come up with was the identification of a high school to be closed and demolished, the closing of another with no plan for the vacant building; and the board's normal amount of neglect as the plan for the remaining facilities. The saying, having no plan is planning to fail, is a fit mantra for what the board has done to date. The following is copied directly from HACC's RFP.

*"This is the most critical project the college will undertake in the next ten years. **Needs are not being met** with current resource capabilities of the college and that of the Commonwealth of Pennsylvania. While supporting school district and **state funding has decreased,** the college has developed very good financial strategies in order to support the creation and development of selected capital plans, **<u>but future plans must be comprehensive, taking all factors into consideration.</u>" Emphasis added!*

The aforementioned can replace "the College" with the school district, as it certainly illustrates what is needed in this district. The Harrisburg RFP is in a note book three inches thick containing a hundred pages. That is just the RFP. It is very comprehensive because the college (hopefully the school district's board) clearly understands the importance of planning, phasing and implementation.

Dr. Paullin Altruistically Ready to Help WBASD

Dr. Robert Paullin submitted to the board's facility committee and superintendent a power point presentation outlining his protocol for a successful project. He made an offer to fly to NEPA here to speak with the board at no charge. His protocol was developed and implemented in other districts by international consultant Dr. Robert Paullin.

The following is representative of the salient parts of the presentation as it makes the point. The complete version is available upon request. Side bar: The reason this process was outlined is that there is a major need for master planning and impact studies prior to board actions. This is described below.

Respectively, 5my 0 years' experience submits that:

The educational plan, site location and building site put forth by the WBASB are profoundly educationally deficient, dangerous at its highest level, and costly to a point of potential district bankruptcy. As validated by scholarly research, the WBA's own studies, PFM Inc. five other states, the Hazleton school District, the Scranton School district; the inertia of this project requires the expenditure of a quarter of a billion dollars for a third of the district's students.

These factors coupled with continuing nepotism, cronyism, lack of accountability, etc. makes the actions of the WBA School Board those that one would expect from the worst school board in the state if not the nation. We could do better if we wanted to do better.

To further make my point, permit me to paraphrase Einstein: If you always listen to whom you always listen to, you will always get what you always got. Learning about a former board president who also served as vice president by unanimous vote following very negative media reports posted last year may be at least a partial explanation why this district is in such trouble. Two Face Book posts on her willingness to listen to constituents. There is little question that other board members get upset when the public or news media is in opposition with their views and actions. Sometimes we have to call a duck a duck.

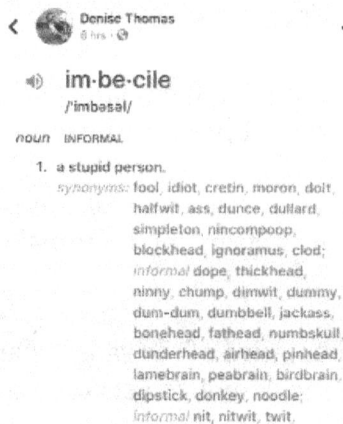

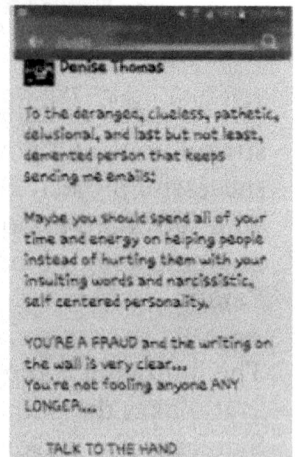

I know that although the state's Plan Con rules requires community input, board members do not like anyone disagreeing with their decrees. The board president who also chaired the board's facility committee rejected a respected member's valuable suggestion. They did not properly vet Dr. Schiowitz, a member of the community— here are his exact words, "he has a plan." It was and still is a plan—

more than the board president can say. The plan maintains the neighborhood schools and expands the concept, while saving the taxpayer's a hundred million dollars.

The board prez threatened Dr. Holodick to state you have a choice-- the board or the Save Our Schools Group.

The need for planning and the answer to "Is there a better way to govern our public-school districts," needs to be addressed. How has the media portrayed WBASD. Here are a set of headlines from the local papers:

Wilkes-Barre Area needs a plan that does not discriminate against most disadvantaged children

W-B Area spent $4.9M on failed school plan

GUEST COMMENTARY

chool board plunging W-B Area into astronomical debt

New legislative report: WB Area has area's highest charter school enrollment

Corruption taints W-B Area board

ETHIC

WILKES-BARRE AREA

SCHOOL BOARD

Wilkes-Barre Area needs a plan that does not discriminate against most disadvantaged children

Moral failure in the W-B Area School District

Recent charges against four Wilkes-Barre Area educators related to alleged improper sexual relationships between teachers and students — some proven, some yet to be adjudicated — surely stem principally from serious individual moral failings. But as they are also a product of the dishonesty and duplicity shown by some of the district's leaders at the times the offenses allegedly occurred.

The alleged transgressions, which include sex with minors and/or failure to report such incidents as well as participation in student drinking parties, occurred between 2004 and 2009. Three members of the school board during that period would subsequently plead guilty in connection with illegal payments for contracting and hiring decisions.

The longtime district solicitor would later be accused of swindling clients and overcharging the district, but ques-

Our Voice

tions of his competency precluded a trial before his death. It is difficult to believe that rumors of the bad behavior attributed to the educators at the time did not reach someone in a position of leadership in the district, given the sordid nature of the allegations and the number of students who were apparently aware of them. And it seems obvious that district leaders engaged in their own illegal activities would be much less likely to pursue allegations

There is a wider lesson here also for the voting public: Character matters when placing people in office and choosing untrustworthy leaders at any level of government can have dire, real-life consequences.

of wrongdoing by others. During a sentencing in Luzerne County Court last week, one of the former students victimized by a teacher told a former administrator who neglected to report her abuse that he had failed her.

"Your job was to protect me and you chose to protect the wrong person. In turn, the whole course of my life changed," she said.

The moral failure goes beyond the individual educators. The leadership of the district at the time must bear some responsibility for fostering a culture in which any district employee would even think of not reporting such a situation in order to protect a colleague.

There is a wider lesson here also for the voting public: Character matters when placing people in office and choosing untrustworthy leaders at any level of government can have dire, real-life consequences.

Shakeup overdue for school district

Wilkes-Barre Area school director charged with drunken driving

Police said Ned Evans was transported to Wilkes-Barre General Hospital for a blood-alcohol test. While at the hospital, Evans became **uncooperative and belligerent**, asked to speak with an attorney, and **insulted Fuches, Prokopchak** and hospital security staff, the complaint says. Evans continued to belittle the officers, calling them a specific body part and saying they would be hearing from his attorney, according to the complaint. Evans claimed he was manhandled in the parking lot, wanted hospital staff to take pictures of the back of his bicep, and told Fuches, **"That his left (expletive NUT) has more responsibility that Fuches' entire body."** Police allege in the complaint Evans called Fuches a **"Bully and ruffian. (Fuches) was one of those mean cops you read about on Facebook. All you bald cops are the same, you're just bullies." Walk proud Wilkes-Barre School board!**

Submitted Planning Summary

The final portion of this chapter captures the essence of a PowerPoint presentation submitted by Dr. Paullin to the Wilkes-Barre Area School Board. At the time, the district was in the process of addressing major concerns and challenges that border on upheavals. In fact that still describes the state of affairs at the WBASD fairly accurately.

The children (students) of Wilkes-Barre area are at the forefront as the safety and their proper education is what all of the discussion is about. Practicability decrees that there must be a protocol to address challenges of this magnitude; an order of progression setting priorities as to what needs to be addressed and in what order. Unfortunately, the board in practice does not appear to believe in a proper planning regimen to precede major building activity.

A conceivable order ought to be :

- credibility of authority (school board);
- curricula need based on student achievement
- demographics and interest;
- evaluation of facility requirements based on curriculum;assessment of district wide facilities and ability to meet curricular requirements
- a forensic review of the district's ability to fund the needs coupled with research on potential funding public and private foundations

That is a mouthful my dear readers but all ingredients are necessary to create the right planning and implementation stew.

The point arrived at by January 2020, was an investment of a quarter of a million dollars. It seemed to some to satisfy their major concern - - the 2400 secondary students. Why invest so much?

There are serious concerns in multiple areas:

- About student achievement
- The changing demographics of a changing student population

A state-of-the-art school will not solve the student achievement problem without changes or perhaps better said, without the formation of a proper long term educational plan. With such neglect for years, no doubt the solutions will be costly. This begs the question: "What comes first student achievement or facilities?" Is this a tough question?

The pages that follow prioritize actions by the district. They ensure credibility and support by including internal and external factors in addressing the issues. They also supporting the board of education when it decides to make the changes necessary to best meet the needs of our children in this district/

What is the need?

The importance of involving internal staff cannot be overstated. First is the fact that they do walk the walk, second, it is human nature to support what you have. These individuals and / or groups must have input on what is happening and they must work to complete the initiative. Third, the interaction of discussing this important topic between teachers, administrators and parents can be very positive and should not be minimized.

The following pages in the Paullin presentation lay out the committees responsibilities, and the final report to the board.

ADMINISTRAIVE REVIEW

A CITIZENS' TASK FORCE

Certain people must be trained properly for this a special mission Who should be on this task force. It should be a select group consisting of Stake Holders from the community—especially those who have not had direct involvement with the district for three years or more; It should also include city officials, parents, merchants, industrialist, bankers, law enforcement, clergy, and senior citizens, etc. More people than you might believe are interested. And, remember, they are all taxpayers.

For the purpose of brevity, the following pages from the report omitted are the procedures and the report by the citizens task force.

A DISTRICT WIDE MASTER PLAN

THE AFOREMENTIONED ACTIVITEIS ARE THE FOUNDATIO FOR THE DEVELOPMENT OF A DISTRICT WIDE MASTER PLAN. THE PROJECTED GOAL IS TO FIRST ESTABLISH THE CURRICULA NEEDS OF THE DISTRICT ASTHE CURRICULUM DRIVES THE FACILITY, EQUIPMENT AND STAFFING NEEDS. IN THE PRESENT SITUATION THE FACILITIES ARE DRIVING TO SOME EXTENT THE CURRICULM AS PER THE FINDINGS IN THE PFM REPORT. A MASTER PLAN ESTABLISHES the target and the means.

CONCLUSION

There are pages of recommended actions that are extensive, time consuming and expensive. Of course.

In view of the depth of the challenges facing the district that go well beyond aging facilities, that will indeed near the HALF BILLION DOLLAR mark. There are issues of student achievement, existing families/students, cyber and charter schools and demographics of a changing student population, and fiscal limitations that will thus be extensive, time consuming and expensive to address and correct. Expect no less.

The bottom line is two-fold:

1. Create a Comprehensive Education Plan Plan

2. Work the plan to a successful conclusion

Chapter 19 Final Thoughts on WBA Public School Governance

Wilkes-Barre Area School District
Governed by the
Wilkes-Barre Are School Board

Here are a few questions, the answers to which are necessary for the problems to be solved:

- **What happened?**
- **Why did it happen?**
- **How can we fix it?**

Does the riposte answer the following question,

"Is this the best we can do in governing public schools?"

Let's begin the tackling job that this dilemma presents. What happened here is a mountain of errors and omissions. The apparent victims doubled down on the problem by not holding the leadership, the people, and the agencies accountable. It happened because as most things do: "we always did it that way."

We can fix it only by first identifying and admitting there are major issues in governing and administering the daily operation of a school district named The Wilkes-Barre Area School District and the inability to recognize the intrinsic value and the protocol of planning per se, and educational planning in particular.

The current board as well as previous WBA boards have not understood nor fully comprehended the mammoth impairment to the quality of education for our children caused by their actions and the nepotism, cronyism, and favoritism that preceded those actions. With the wrong team of horses, even the Pony Express won't get the mail delivered. And, so the selection of the team cannot be left to the spoils system.

The importance of planning pointed out by research and the PFM study, the importance of a curriculum designed as part of the plan to meet the needs of the students we serve--with the same curriculum dictating facility needs cannot be overestimated. Despite The evident priority of sports over academics, board leadership must perform its mission to form the proper balance between all competing needs.

And, of course as we have seen in this district, the damaging practice of ignoring the scholarly research, the district's own past and present studies, experiences of surrounding school districts, and input from the community pays huge negative consequences that take over and become the de facto plan for the future. Not only does ignoring academic deficiencies' cause students to flee the district, but implementing known factors that lower academic achievements, increase and promote such exodus as the WBA constituents seek what is best for them.

Closing neighborhood schools, school isolation, consolidation, reduction of varsity sports and extracurricular activities, clubs; extensive bussing; reducing instructional time, and removing by distance the parents' ability to be involved in their children's activities and instruction contribute to a district malaise—what's the use???

On top of all the problems in the poor governance afflicting the Wilkes-Barre Area School District it still needs to again be pointed out that building a school on the worst, most costly, most toxic, subsidence prone, 78 acres in the entire county has its consequences. The credibility of the past boards is at the bottom, the present plan— overpayment for a toxic site, potential debt, arrogance, and social media posts are very damaging to this board because the board brought this set of circumstances upon themselves by being unresponsive to the real needs of the community it serves.

Please let me conclude this treatise with a quote/opinion from the PFM study: "Either the board does not see the threat, or they don't care."

Other Books by Brian W. Kelly : (amazon.com, and Kindle)

The Corruption in the Wilkes-Barre Area School District--about toxic corruption and stinky things
Stolen Election ??? Democrats say: "fair and just;" Republican cowards surrender to Democrats
The Ten Commandments of Calipered Kinematically Aligned Total Knee Arthroplasty Color Edit.
The Ten Commandments of Calipered Kinematically Aligned Total Knee Arthroplasty B/W Edition
About Alexa! Tell me how!
Chronicle of Inept Governance & Corrective Actions from a school board from hell
Hey Alexa! Create me my own personal musical paradise
The Big Toxic School at Little Chernobyl Unpublished with new book (Corruption in WBASD)
FTC Case: LetsGoPublish.com v Amazon Fourth Edition big bully censored nine books
FTC Case: LetsGoPublish.com v Amazon Third Edition big bully censored nine books
FTC Case: LetsGoPublish.com v Amazon Second Edition big bully censored nine books
The President Donald J. Trump Book Catalog Color Version by Brian Kelly & Lets Go Publish!
The President Donald J. Trump Book Catalog B/W Version by Brian Kelly & Lets Go Publish!
FTC Case: LetsGoPublish.com v Amazon Original case bully censored nine books
What America Wins if Biden Wins Everything!!!!!! The answer is really nothing.
What America Loses if Trump Loses None of the 1000s of Trump wins for starters
What America Wins When Trump Wins Trump already gave the country more benefits and blessings
We Love Trump! Don't you? The President given to the people by God as the answer to our prayers
Amazon: The Biggest Bully in Town bully blocked eight books in 2020 by most published author
Trump Assured 2020 Victory President needs these two prongs for his platform for landslide
2020 Republican Convention—Speeches Blocked by Amazon Includes memento free Link
2020 RNC Convention Full Speech Transcripts Blocked by Amazon Memento of the 87 best
COVID-19 Mask, Yes? Or No? It's Everybody's Recommended Solution!!!
LSU Tigers Championship Seasons Starts at beginning of LSU Football to the National Championship
Great Coaches in LSU Football Book starts with the first LSU coach; goes to Orgeron Championship
Great Players in LSU Football Begins with 1893 QB Ruffin G Pleasant to 2019 QB Burrow
America for Millennialsl A growing # of disintegrationists want to tear US down
Great Moments in LSU Football Book starts at start of Football to the Ed Orgeron Championship.
The Constitution's Role in a Return to Normalcy Can the Constitution Survive?
The Constitution vs. The Virus Simultaneous attack coronavirus and US governors
One, Two, Three, Pooph!!! Reopen Country Now! Return to normalcy is just around the corner.
Reopen America Now Return to Normalcy
Enough is Enough!Re Re: Covid, We are not children. We're adults.We'll make the right decisions.
How to Write Your 1st Book & Publish it Using Amazon KDP You can do it
REMDESIVIR A Ray of Hope
When Will America Reopen for Business? This author's opinion includes voices of experts
HydroxyChloroquine: The Game Changer
Super Bowl & NFL Championship Seasons The KC Chiefs From the 1st to Super Bowl LIV
Great Coaches in Kansas City Chiefs Football First Coach era to Andy Reid Era
Great Players in Kansas City Chiefs Football From the AFL to Andy Reid Era
Reopen America Now! How to Shut-Down Corona Virus & Return to Normalcy!
Why is Everybody Moving to the Villages? You can afford a home in the Villages
CORONAVIRUS The Cause & the Cure. Many solutions—but which ones will work?
Great Moments in Kansas City Chiefs Football. From the beginning to the Andy Reid Era
How the Philadelphia Eagles Lost Its Karma. This is the one place that tells the story
Cancel All Student Debt Now! Good for America, Good for the Economy.
Social Security Screw Job!!! Scandal: Seniors Intentionally Screwed by US Government
Trump Hate They hate Trump Supporters; Trump; & God—in that order
Christmas Wings for Brian A heartwarming story of a boy whose shoulders kept growing
Merry Christmas to Wilkes-Barre 50 Ways" for Mayor George Brown to Create a Better City.
Air Force Football Championship Seasons From AF Championship to Coach Calhoun's teams
Syracuse Football Championship Seasons beginning of SU championships; goes to Dino Babers Era
Navy Football Championship Seasons 1st Navy Championships to the Ken Niumatalolo Era
Army Football Championship Seasons Beginning of Football championships to Jeff Monken Era
Florida Gators Championship Seasons Beginning of Football & championships to Dan Mullen era
Alabama's Championship Seasons Beginning of Football past the 2018 National Championship
Clemson Tigers Championship Seasons Beginning of Football to the Clemson Natl Championships
Penn State's Championship Seasons PSU's first championship to the James Franklin era
Notre Dame's Championship Seasons Before Knute Rockne and past Lou Holtz's 1988 title
Super Bowls & Championship Seasons: The New York Giants Many championships of the Giants.
Super Bowls & Championship Seasons: New England Patriots Many championships of the Patriots.
Super Bowls & Championship Seasons: The Pittsburgh Steelers Many championship of the Steelers
Super Bowls & Championship Seasons: The Philadelphia Eagles Many championships of the Eagles.
The Big Toxic School Wilkes-Barre Area's Tale of Corruption, Deception, Taxation & Tyranny

Great Players in New York Giants Football Begins with great players of 1925 to the Saquon Barqley.
Great Coaches in New York Giants Football Begins with Bob Folwell 1925 and to Pat Shurmur 2019.
Great Moments in New York Giants Football Beginning of Football to the Pat Shurmur era.
Hasta La Vista California Give California its independence.
IT's ALL OVER! Mueller: "NO COLLUSION!"—Top Dems going to jail for the hoax!
Democrat Secret for Power & Winning Elections Open borders adds millions of new Dem Voters
Hope for Wilkes-Barre—John Q. Doe—Next Mayor of Wilkes-Barre
The John Doe Plan & WB Plan will help create a better city!
Great Moments in New England Patriots Football Second Edition
This book begins at the beginning of Football and goes to the Bill Belichick era.
The Cowardly Congress Corrupt US Congress is against America and Americans.
Great Players in Air Force Football From the beginning to the current season
Great Coaches in Air Force Football Grom the beginning to Coach Troy Calhoun
Help for Mayor George and Next Mayor of Wilkes-Barre How to vote for the next Mayor Council
Ghost of Wilkes-Barre Future: Spirit's advice for residents how to pick the next Mayor and Council
Great Players in Air Force Football: Air Force's best players of all time
Great Coaches in Air Force Football: From Coach 1 to Coach Troy Calhoun
Great Moments in Air Force Football: From day 1 to today
Great Players in Navy Football: Navy's best including Bellino & Staubach
Great Coaches in Navy Football: From Coach 1 to Coach #39 Ken Niumatalolo
Great Moments in Navy Football: From day 1 to coach Ken Niumatalolo l
No Tree! No Toys! No Toot! Heartwarming story. Christmas gone while 19 month old napped
How to End DACA, Sanctuary Cities, & Resident Illegal Aliens . best solution remove shadows.
Government Must Stop Ripping Off Seniors' Social Security!: Hey buddy, seniors can't spare a dime?
Special Report: Solving America's Student Debt Crisis!: The only real solution to the $1.52 Trillion
The Winning Political Platform for America Unique winning approach solve problems in America.
Lou Barletta v Bob Casey for US Senate Barletta's unique approach to solve big problems in America.
John Chrin v Matt Cartwright for Congress Chrin has a unique approach to solve problems
The Cure for Hate !!! Can the cure be any worse than this disease that is crippling America?
Andrew Cuomo's Time to Go? "He Was Never that Great!": Cuomo says America never that great
White People Are Bad! Bad! Bad! Whoever thought a popular slogan in 2018 *It's OK to be White!*
The Fake News Media Is Also Corrupt !!!: Fake press / media today is not worthy to be 4th Estate.
God Gave US Donald Trump? Trump was sent from God as the people's answer
Millennials Say America Was "Never That Great": Too many pleased days political chumps not over!
It's Time for The John Q. Doe Party… Don't you think? By Elephants.
Great Players in Florida Gators Football… Tim Tebow and a ton of other great players
Great Coaches in Florida Gators Football… The best coaches in Gator history.
The Constitution by Hamilton, Jefferson, Madison, et al. The Real Constitution
The Constitution Companion. Will help you learn and understand the Constitution
Great Coaches in Clemson Football The best Clemson Coaches right to Dabo Swinney
Great Players in Clemson Football The best Clemson players in history
Winning Back America. America's been stolen and can be won back completely
The Founding of America… Great book to pick up a lot of great facts
Defeating America's Career Politicians. The scoundrels need to go.
Midnight Mass by Jack Lammers… You remember what it was like Great story
The Bike by Jack Lammers… Great heartwarming Story by Jack
Wipe Out All Student Loan Debt--Now! Watch the economy go boom!
No Free Lunch Pay Back Welfare! Why not pay it back?
Deport All Millennials Now!!! Why they deserve to be deported and/or saved
DELETE the EPA, Please! The worst decisions to hurt America
Taxation Without Representation 4th Edition Should we throw the TEA overboard again?
Four Great Political Essays by Thomas Dawson
Top Ten Political Books for 2018… Cliffnotes Version of 10 Political Books
Top Six Patriotic Books for 2018… Cliffnotes version of 6 Patriotic Boosk
Why Trump Got Elected!.. It's great to hear about a great milestone in America!
The Day the Free Press Died. Corrupt Press Lives on!
Solved (Immigration) The best solutions for 2018
Solved II (Obamacare, Social Security, Student Debt) Check it out; They're solved.
Great Moments in Pittsburgh Steelers Football… Six Super Bowls and more.
Great Players in Pittsburgh Steelers Football ,,,Chuck Noll, Bill Cowher, Mike Tomin, etc.
Great Coaches in New England Patriots Football,,, Bill Belichick the one and only plus others
Great Players in New England Patriots Football… Tom Brady, Drew Bledsoe et al.
Great Coaches in Philadelphia Eagles Football..Andy Reid, Doug Pederson & Lots more
Great Players in Philadelphia Eagles Football Great players such as Sonny Jurgenson
Great Coaches in Syracuse Football All the greats including Ben Schwartzwalder
Great Players in Syracuse Football. Highlights best players such as Jim Brown & Donovan McNabb
Millennials are People Too !!! Give US millennials help to live American Dream
Brian Kelly for the United States Senate from PA: Fresh Face for US Senate

The Candidate's Bible. Don't pray for your campaign without this bible
Rush Limbaugh's Platform for Americans... Rush will love it
Sean Hannity's Platform for Americans... Sean will love it
Donald Trump's New Platform for Americans. Make Trump unbeatable in 2020
Tariffs Are Good for America! One of the best tools a president can have
Great Coaches in Pittsburgh Steelers Football Sixteen of the best coaches ever to coach in pro football.
Great Moments in New England Patriots Football Great football moments from Boston to NE
Great Moments in Philadelphia Eagles Football. The best from the Eagles from the beginning Great
Moments in Syracuse Football The great moments, coaches & players in Syracuse Football
Boost Social Security Now! Hey Buddy Can You Spare a Dime?
The Birth of American Football. From the first college game in 1869 to the last Super Bowl
Obamacare: A One-Line Repeal Congress must get this done.
A Wilkes-Barre Christmas Story A wonderful town makes Christmas all the better
A Boy, A Bike, A Train, and a Christmas Miracle A Christmas story that will melt your heart
Pay-to-Go America-First Immigration Fix
Legalizing Illegal Aliens Via Resident Visas Americans-first plan saves $Trillions. Learn how!
60 Million Illegal Aliens in America!!! A simple, America-first solution.
The Bill of Rights By Founder James Madison Refresh *your knowledge of the specific rights for all*
Great Players in Army Football Great Army Football played by great players..
Great Coaches in Army Football Army's coaches are all great.
Great Moments in Army Football Army Football at its best.
Great Moments in Florida Gators Football Gators Football from the start. This is the book.
Great Moments in Clemson Football CU Football at its best. This is the book.
Great Moments in Florida Gators Football Gators Football from the start. This is the book.
The Constitution Companion. A Guide to Reading and Comprehending the Constitution
The Constitution by Hamilton, Jefferson, & Madison – Big type and in English
PATERNO: The Dark Days After Win # 409. Sky began to fall within days of win # 409.
JoePa 409 Victories: Say No More! Winningest Division I-A football coach ever
American College Football: The Beginning From before day one football was played.
Great Coaches in Alabama Football Challenging the coaches of every other program!
Great Coaches in Penn State Football the Best Coaches in PSU's football program
Great Players in Penn State Football The best players in PSU's football program
Great Players in Notre Dame Football The best players in ND's football program
Great Coaches in Notre Dame Football The best coaches in any football program
Great Players in Alabama Football from Quarterbacks to offensive Linemen Greats!
Great Moments in Alabama Football AU Football from the start. This is the book.
Great Moments in Penn State Football PSU Football, start--games, coaches, players,
Great Moments in Notre Dame Football ND Football, start, games, coaches, players
Cross Country with the Parents A great trip from East Coast to West with the kids
Seniors, Social Security & the Minimum Wage. Things seniors need to know.
How to Write Your First Book and Publish It with CreateSpace. You too can be an author.
The US Immigration Fix--It's all in here. Finally, an answer.
I had a Dream IBM Could be #1 Again The title is self-explanatory
WineDiets.Com Presents The Wine Diet Learn how to lose weight while having fun.
Wilkes-Barre, PA; Return to Glory Wilkes-Barre City's return to glory
Geoffrey Parsons' Epoch... The Land of Fair Play Better than the original.
The Bill of Rights 4 Dummmies! This is the best book to learn about your rights.
Sol Bloom's Epoch ...Story of the Constitution The best book to learn the Constitution
America 4 Dummmies! All Americans should read to learn about this great country.
The Electoral College 4 Dummmies! How does it really work?
The All-Everything Machine Story about IBM's finest computer server.
ThankYou IBM! This book explains how IBM was beaten in the computer marketplace by neophytes

Amazon.com/author/brianwkelly
Brian W. Kelly has written 250 books including this one.
Thank you for buying this one.
Others can be found at amazon.com/author/brianwkelly